WHODUNIT ? ? ?

- **?** The designing woman who lost her clothes
- **?** The victim's half-Indian son and heir
- **?** The fickle fiancée
- **?** The mysterious museum manager
- **?** Woodrow Wilson

They were all suspects—and they all kept getting in Inspector Cramer's hair as he wove a web for the real killer!

The Adventures of Nero Wolfe

BLACK ORCHIDS
FER-DE-LANCE
NOT QUITE DEAD ENOUGH
OVER MY DEAD BODY
THE RED BOX
THE RUBBER BAND
SOME BURIED CAESAR
TOO MANY CROOKS
THE LEAGUE OF FRIGHTENED MEN

Other Mysteries

BAD FOR BUSINESS
THE BROKEN VASE
DOUBLE FOR DEATH
THE HAND IN THE GLOVE
RED THREADS
THE SOUND OF MURDER
(orig. title: *Alphabet Hicks*)
THE PRESIDENT VANISHES

These Rex Stout mysteries are published by Pyramid Books.

RED THREADS

REX STOUT

PYRAMID BOOKS ▲ NEW YORK

RED THREADS

A PYRAMID BOOK
Published by arrangement with the author

Farrar & Rinehart Mystery Book edition published 1939
Pyramid edition published November, 1964
   Second printing July, 1967
   Third printing January, 1969

Copyright, 1939, 1967, by Rex Stout
All Rights Reserved

Printed in the United States of America

  PYRAMID BOOKS are published by Pyramid Publications, Inc.
  444 Madison Avenue, New York, New York 10022, U.S.A.

I

Eileen Delaney heard the door of the noisy old elevator close behind her, and the diminuendo of its bang and rattle as its ascent progressed up the shaft. A few steps down the hall she was confronted by a dingy glass-paneled door bearing the inscription in gilt-edged black lettering:

JEAN FARRIS FABRICS, INC.

Entrance

Before turning the knob and entering, she glared at the legend and stuck out her tongue at it. This implied no hatred of Jean Farris or enmity toward fabrics; the fact was that she admired the one to excess and permitted the other to monopolize all her talents and attention; the derisive protrusion of her tongue was merely a private but visible recording of her skeptical attitude toward life in general and her intention to keep her sense of proportion even upon entering a shrine. Especially since she was a stockholder in the shrine.

Tossing a nod on the fly at the chunky little woman seated at a flat-topped desk in the anteroom, Miss Delaney went on through another door in a partition. There was noise and activity, and even bustle. It was an enormous room, running the entire length of the building, and its width at least a third of its length. Beams of wooden-framed structures, nine feet high and nearly as wide, made a confusing maze of horizontal and vertical lines, and the confusion was completed by arrays of countless spools on spindles, taut threads of yarns converging on their slots in steel guides, shuttles gliding rapidly back and forth with the woof to be imprisoned in the warp, and the movements of the men and women on their stools before the looms. But there were no racing belts and no whirring of machinery; these were hand looms.

Miss Delaney went down the broad aisle, halting for a moment beside a loom where a woman with black hair, dark skin, and a strong straight back sat on the stool whipping the shuttle, and then continuing almost to the other end, where a worried-looking middle-aged man who was smoking a pipe advanced to greet her.

Miss Delaney said, "Hello, Karl. Everything will smell of tobacco again."

He kept the pipe in his mouth and said with a meekness that was veneered on iron, "I think not. You know the sponging."

"I know. All right. Why have you put Pakahle on the piece for Muir & Beebe? I thought you agreed—"

"Pakahle is a fine weaver."

"Sure she is, but on heavy stuff. She'll never in God's world keep that piece tight enough."

"She will. Jake is home, sick. I watch her."

"You'd better. You know—if it comes back—" Miss Delaney shrugged. "What I wanted to tell you, Krone says he must have the natural kasha, the one with nubs, by tomorrow afternoon. He has sold it to a giraffe named Mrs. Richmond for a sports ensemble, and she keeps telephoning from Newport and reversing the charge. Can you make it?"

"I think so."

"Good. I'll phone Krone and relieve his mind." Miss Delaney turned to go, then she wheeled on him again and lifted her nose for an offensive sniff. "If you told me that's thyme and rosemary in that pipe, I still wouldn't like it."

She left him. Returning half the length of the broad aisle, and crossing to the far side, she passed through a door set in a ceiling-high glassed partition. This was apparently a storage room, with two large tables, enclosed shelves and bins, and a strong smell of naphthalene. There were other doors at either end, and Miss Delaney headed for the one on the left. She rapped with her knuckles on its panel, and then immediately opened it and went in, involuntarily inhaling for the breath of a sigh as she did so.

She always sighed on entering that room, though she had come to realize that its chaos resulted not so much from disorder as from the laws of space. Untold thousands of skeins and windings and spools of yarn—linen, silk, cotton, wool, alpaca, cashmere, Shetland, mohair, llama—were on shelves, stands and tables, draped on the backs of chairs, hung in loops on the walls. Also on the walls were color charts, squares and rectangles of fabrics, sketches, drawings, whole pieces of materials, prints of ancient textiles, and various unclassifiable objects. Other yarns and fabrics were in bags and boxes and baskets on shelves and tables and the floor; and on the largest table was a clutter of sheets of paper of all sizes, crayons and pencils, scissors and glue and other miscellany, and more yarns and shreds of fabric.

At one side of this table a young woman was perched on a high stool. She had soft hair the color of strained honey, gray eyes whose lids came to a point with a faint upthrust toward the temples, and highly colored cheeks; and wore a blue linen smock which was not especially clean. What she had been doing was uncertain, for as the intruder entered she appeared to be completing some quick, rather flurried movement, and made a grab for one of the sheets of paper.

Miss Delaney gazed at her in astonishment. "Well, now what?" She advanced to the table. "I swear to God you're blushing!"

Jean Farris laughed and swung around on the stool. "Of course I'm blushing! Your knock startled me. I was reading that article by Stuart. I'm not conceited enough to swallow that. Have you read it?"

Miss Delaney grunted, with a doubtful eye. "You're conceited enough. For more than that. Anyway, I don't see it— Oh, under there?" She took two steps. "Why did you hide —" She reached for a pile of skeins, and under it. Jean Farris put out a hand at her, and hastily drew it back. Miss Delaney's hand emerged from the pile of skeins clutching a book. "But Stuart's article wasn't in a— What the dickens is this?" She flipped back the cover and frowned at the title page, held the frown for some seconds, finally tossed the book back onto the table, looked sharply at Jean Farris's face, still highly colored, and let out a snort.

"So!" There was a suggestion of a squeak in her voice. "I don't suppose you were reading Stuart's article in that book?"

Jean said mildly, "I—I didn't mean I was reading it that minute—when you came in. I read it this morning. He said that my color sense, combined with my feeling for—"

"I know he did. Excuse me. It was that book that you shoved under the yarn when I came in. *Customs and Culture of the Cherokee Indians*. I suppose ethnology is very interesting, but good heavens! You hid the book when you heard me coming, and I never saw you blush like that."

"I didn't hide it."

"Certainly you hid it."

"I wasn't blushing. If I was, it was only because I'm a week late on those designs for the Oxford and Shetland—"

"You're always late. It never matters, because everyone is more than willing to wait till you're ready, and you ought to be ashamed of yourself to intimate that I would ever have the nerve to get impatient—"

Miss Delaney stopped because she realized that her voice was squeaky. She turned for a chair, acquired one by moving a box of color cards from its seat to a stand, and sat down.

She looked into the young woman's gray eyes. "We might as well not be silly. May I ask you a question, Jean? Where did you get that book and why were you reading it? Just an ordinary question."

"I got it—" Jean waved a hand, vaguely. Then she grinned. "I got it at the oddest place! You'd never guess. A bookstore! And I'm reading it because I am a designer of fabrics—Jean Farris, maybe you've heard the name?—and there is a great deal to be learned from the study of primitive weaving. . . . I think it is pretty darned honest of me to admit that I still need to learn. . . ."

Miss Delaney, looking straight at her, snorted again. She said grimly, "You really should know better than to try to fake me."

"Why, Eileen! I wouldn't! You know very well I'm interested in the American Indian design and workmanship! Didn't I spend two weeks in New Mexico, and didn't I bring Pakahle back with me?"

"Pakahle is a Navajo. The Cherokees couldn't weave a gunny sack—and anyhow, they never tried." Miss Delaney shook her head, with compressed lips. "No. You shouldn't try to fake me, Jean. I know all about it anyway. It's obvious. I've suspected it ever since Saturday, when you went to that ball game. Why in the name of heaven should you go to a ball game? Romance." Miss Delaney snorted. "You went to all the trouble of buying that book, and sitting there reading about the customs of a bunch of savages that couldn't even weave, and you tried to hide the book when I caught you at it, and you blushed like a sunset on a post card because I caught you. . . . Why? Because the worst thing that could possibly happen has happened. You haven't even fallen in love with a man. You have gone dotty over a damned aborigine."

"I have not gone dotty!"

"You have gone dotty. A Cherokee Indian."

"Adam and Eve were aborigines!"

"That's ridiculous. Anyway, if we're discussing romance, the less said about Adam and Eve the better. You know what happened to theirs."

"I didn't mention romance, you did. Will Rogers was a Cherokee Indian."

"I never met him. It's a good thing you didn't. So you don't deny it?"

"Of course not." Jean's cheeks had hoisted a flag again, but not this time, apparently, the banner of embarrassment. Her gray eyes looked indignant. "Really, Eileen. I don't feel under the necessity of denying or admitting anything."

"Meaning it's none of my business." Miss Delaney compressed her lips and sat motionless for a full minute. A keen eye might have perceived that the lips were not compressed quite tightly enough, might have remarked a faint inclination to sag at the corners; but if a streak of pathos, a concealed doubt of her ability to avert impending calamity, did indeed adulterate her resolution, it was not apparent in her voice. She resumed, "But you're wrong, you know you are. I certainly don't pretend to be an expert on lovers, though I'm fifty-two years old, which is exactly twice your age. Lack of experience. But I'm an expert on you. You have the finest and most original talent for textile design in America—if Marley Stuart says so, why shouldn't I, even if I am your partner? And you not only have the talent, you have a passion for it. It's a strange and beautiful fire in you; it actually creates things that didn't exist before; and a century from now, two centuries, more, men and women will wear things on their backs that will be different from what they would have been if you hadn't lived."

Jean said, "Piffle. I just like to make designs."

"Lots of other people like to, too. Don't be modest. You know darned well how good you are, you have too much sense not to. So if anything happened to take you away from this"—Miss Delaney's head pivoted for a survey of the rainbow chaos of the room—"it would be a disaster for humanity. Not as big a disaster as the end of the world maybe, but it would be an awful shame. So if you go dotty over a Cherokee Indian, it's everybody's business, and it is particularly my business because I'm personally and selfishly concerned. I've been bumming around the textile and fashion world for thirty years now, in various capacities, and it wasn't until I tied up with you, four years ago, that I got anything out of it except three meals a day—when I wasn't reducing—and the trick of keeping my fingers crossed during business hours. Look at them now."

She extended a hand and wiggled the fingers. "I've forgotten how. You, nothing but an inspired kid, you've made an honest woman of me. I could get maudlin easy, you know I'm Irish. So to me it would be worse than a disaster if you were to give this up; it would mean diving back into that mess—"

"But, Eileen! I haven't the faintest intention of giving it up! My lord, just because I read a book on the customs and culture of the Cherokee Indians—"

"That's not it." Miss Delaney sounded gloomy. "I mean, look at you. I can't imagine how you've escaped both the altar and the bed of sin as long as you have. With your—well, your physical construction and appearance—a man is not only probable, he's inevitable, and humanity could have no objection to that, and neither could I. Of course, the ideal would be a good-looking youngster who would understand and appreciate your work and the importance of your career, and would make himself useful—he might give Karl a hand and perhaps eventually take Karl's place, or he might be better fitted for the promotion end and help me out—possibly even business manager. . . ."

"My God." Jean shuddered. Then she laughed. "I thought you spoke of romance."

"I did." Miss Delaney sounded stubborn. "I swear you're an innocent—you, who studied five years in Vienna! A romance with a salesman or a bookkeeper can get just as good results as one with an Indian, on the average better. I have nothing against romance. The truth is, I have nothing against Indians either. If you happened to focus on one like Mabel Dodge's Tony, I would be delighted. We could get him a big cushion to sit on and find room to put it somewhere—even in this room with you if you wanted to. What I don't like—and I maintain it is my business, and a lot of other people's—is your getting lightheaded over the chance to become a quote lady unquote and go to hell."

Jean laughed again. "I wouldn't be a lady if you gave it to me for nothing. There might be some excitement in hell—"

"Not in that one. And you'll be a lady if you marry Guy Carew. Not that I suppose you've gone far enough to consider marriage; I'm trying to catch it in its early stage. Now that his father's dead he's worth perhaps twenty million—possibly twice that. He owns a yacht, a villa at Palm Beach, a place in the Adirondacks, the house on Sixty-ninth Street, the estate of Lucky Hills in Westchester, a racing stable—do you think he'd let you go on sitting on that stool breathing creation or fussing with yarn dealers or arguing with Karl or having your picture took for *Women's Wear Daily?* Or if he did let you, that you'd still be inclined to take the trouble, after a year or so? You would not. You would either rot or dry up. Pieces and shreds of you—"

"Eileen! Stop! I would not. And he isn't like that. He didn't buy the yacht or the Palm Beach villa. He spends his time out West, among his people, the Indians, helping them—"

"You mean he did spend his time like that. It's a good field for a dilettante. He's not a rich man's son now, he's the rich man. I'm not saying he's just a lump of living tissue; though he inherited his millions, I'll admit it's quite possible that he earned them." Miss Delaney snorted. "How long has it been, a month, since his father was murdered? In such a peculiar fashion? And the police appear to be completely up a tree?" She snorted again. "*Appear* to be! But of course you hear the gossip as well as I do. I suppose that might make him more romantic, to have half of New York convinced that he's a parricide—only I wouldn't have thought you'd fall—"

The concentration in Jean's eyes stopped her. She met them, with an effort, in silence. Jean said, low and quiet, "Why . . . that's bad of you. I thought you were only acid sometimes . . . I didn't know you could be venomous. . . ."

"I can be." Miss Delaney was quiet too. "Where any danger to this is concerned. This is my life now, my whole life." She put up a hand as if to touch the other, but the distance was too great, and the hand fell back to her lap. "Only I didn't intend to be venomous, and I don't think I was. After all, you do hear the gossip; I wasn't saying anything new. Honestly, Jean, honestly, I don't want to see you make a mistake. I would do anything to keep you here. Maybe I've made a mistake myself, but surely it can't have gone very far, since you only met the man two weeks ago—and I thought—when I saw you with that book—before it could develop into something serious—"

"I guess it already has." Jean tried a little laugh which didn't work very well. "They say marriage is serious."

"What!" Miss Delaney's squeak was unrestrained. *"Marriage?"*

Jean nodded and repeated firmly, "Marriage."

"You . . . you . . . Jean . . ." The squeak came under control. "I don't believe it. You're just trying to see if I would fall dead. Well, I would."

"No, you won't. It won't affect us—this business. At least, not much."

"I don't believe it. You don't mean it's all settled?"

"Why . . ." Jean hesitated, and her brow showed a wrinkle. "It is and it isn't. Secretly it *is* settled. I mean, I know about it but he doesn't. You've never seen him, have you?"

"No. How does it happen he doesn't know it's settled?"

"Because it hasn't come up." The wrinkle in Jean's brow

was joined by another. "You see . . . you know how I am. I've never been much for men, have I?"

"No, thank God. You've been too busy."

Jean nodded. "I'm not as innocent as you think I am. I've had lots of—I suppose you might call them ideas—about different men—especially the one in Vienna who wanted to give me that mountain I told you about—but whenever it got to a certain point I couldn't help laughing. You know, when they begin to look as if their collar was choking them?"

"I don't know. I don't seem to have that effect on their collars."

"Well, I do . . . that is, I mean, they do look that way, and it isn't possible to keep from laughing, and they get as mad as the devil. Then I suppose, as you say, I've been so interested in my work—"

"Has this Indian begun choking yet?"

"No." Quick blood made spots of color on Jean's cheeks. Her chin lifted. "Nothing has occurred . . . I don't consider him in that connection. I do make quick decisions about things, you know I do. Up till Saturday afternoon I had no idea whether I would ever be married or not; I hadn't thought about it much. Then quite suddenly I decided I would marry him. That's why I say it's settled for me but it hasn't been settled for him yet."

"Has he mentioned the subject?"

"Certainly not. He's only seen me four times."

Miss Delaney sat motionless, with pursed lips, staring with concentrated speculation at her partner's face. Finally she declared with emphasis, "I don't believe it. You're rolling me. You're fairly well educated, and you have a good sense of humor, and there you sit talking like a paleolithic cave girl on leap year day. Unless you're really deep and devious, which I've never suspected, and you've decided in cold blood to freeze onto that twenty million or whatever it is."

Jean was laughing. "I don't care whether he has twenty million or twenty cents! I can always make money, with you to help." She sobered. "But it's settled. Really, Eileen. And don't you dare mention it to *any*body, because I don't know, it may take years— Well! Come in!"

The knock had been at the door in the partition behind her, across the room from the one by which Miss Delaney had entered. It opened, and the chunky little woman from the anteroom appeared, carrying a large flat box of green and yellow cardboard secured with wide yellow tape. She advanced to the table.

"From Krone."

Jean Farris had bounded from the stool and was exclaiming. "Thank heaven! I was afraid it wouldn't get here in time. I'll be late as it is. No, wait, Cora, don't go, I want to see how you like it. You too, Eileen, of course." She had the lid off and the top garment unfolded and was holding it up for inspection. "Oh, my God! He ended that stripe at the wrong—no, he didn't. Look! See how the line of the stripe in the jacket will meet it? Hey, what's that? Oh—snip that thread, will you, Cora? Isn't it pretty fine? Would you think that stripe could be so quiet? That's because the dark blend of the tabby absorbs it—just a trick! Everything is just a trick." She laughed. With the smock off and likewise the dress that had been under it, the pink silk hanging from the shoulder straps left almost as much bare skin displayed as if it had been a fashionable swimming suit. The skin was nicely tanned. She touched the pink silk. "Have you seen these, Eileen? Bretton's are featuring them—they call them Shapesheers! Isn't that terrible? Sheepshears, Shakespeares—it will haunt you. Cora, please dear, the brown pumps from that cupboard—no, over there—I'm glad it isn't sweltering, because I do want to show this sort of casually—and oh, I forgot to phone Roberts & Creel to send samples of that two-sixteens mixture—"

Miss Delaney was emptying a drawer, trying to find stockings to go with the brown pumps.

II

Inspector Cramer removed a shred of cigar from his tongue with his finger and thumb and deposited it in an ash tray on the police commissioner's desk. "I'm not exactly kicking," he declared, "I'm only remarking. I only say, it's not our cat and why should we apologize if we don't skin it? I take a man's-size vacation for the first time in fifteen years, and to get called back like this for something that happened at the North Pole—"

District Attorney Skinner gestured impatiently. "Swallow it, Cramer. You're sore because the fishing wasn't good and the flies bit you. Mount Kisco isn't the North Pole. It's out of our jurisdiction, but District Attorney Anderson of Westchester has asked for help, and the press and the public know we're working on it anyhow, and we're taking it on the chin.

Anyway, here you are. Do you mean to say you haven't read about it?"

"I do." The inspector sounded bitter. "I've been up in Canada branding moose, and as for fish—"

"All right." Skinner was brusque. "Then you'll have to hear all of it. Shall I shoot, Humbert?"

The police commissioner nodded. "Go ahead."

"Okay. I'll condense it as much as I can." Skinner took a thick batch of papers from a folder, laid them on the table, and leaned back in his chair. "I suppose you know the history of Val Carew."

"Some."

"We know it all, now. Thirty-five years ago he was a gambler out in Oklahoma. We haven't picked up anything definite earlier than 1905, when he met an Indian girl, a Cherokee, and married her. They had a son, and lived on the tribal land until 1913, when the oil thing got big and the Indians cleaned up. The Indian girl—her name was Tsianina—her father was a chief and got ten headrights, so he was rich, and he staked Carew and his daughter and they came east, straight to New York. Since Val Carew was a born gambler, he took his stake to Wall Street, where the gambling was good, and within five years, by the time the war ended, he had multiplied his pile by ten and learned all the tricks.

"Ten years ago, in 1927, his wife died. He had introduced her around New York as an Indian princess, and apparently she really was a princess to him, or even, you might say, a goddess, for he worshiped her from the day he married her until the day she died." Skinner rummaged among the papers, withdrew one, and tossed it across. "There's a picture of her. People say she was even more beautiful than that; I never met her. Anyhow, by 1927 Carew was up in the really high brackets, and when his wife died he built a tomb for her out of Oklahoma sandstone on his estate at Lucky Hills, as he called it, up north of Mount Kisco. I've been in it; all of us have, for a special reason. It's as big as a barn. The walls, inside, are covered with Indian relics, and there are cabinets filled with them too. The ceiling is thirty feet high. Stone steps lead up to a stone platform, and on top of the stone platform is a casket made of wood, covered with buckskin, and with a glass top. Inside the casket, in plain view, is Tsianina. You ought to see her."

Cramer grunted. "I ought to be in Canada fishing."

"Oh, forget it. Anyway, there she is. I've seen her. We all have. It sounds grotesque, but it isn't, it's impressive. But how do you like this for grotesque? All along one side, running

14

across the wall in a straight line about twenty feet from the floor, is a row of holes eight inches in diameter. There are 365 holes. All you can see, standing on the floor and looking up, is just a hole; but if you climb a ladder and look directly into one, you find that a cylinder has been chiseled clear through the stone wall, thirty inches thick, and you are looking at daylight. What do you suppose those 365 cylinders were chiseled through that wall for?"

Inspector Cramer shook his head. "Got me. Hell, you could have had this printed and mailed me a copy."

"Yeah. But you should have the picture. As I said, Val Carew was a born gambler, and so naturally was superstitious. Also, he worshiped Tsianina, his wife. Also, the Cherokees were traditionally sun worshipers, and Tsianina's father stuck to many of the old customs which most of his tribe had discarded. I've had a lot of this from Amory Buysse, curator of the National Indian Museum; you'll meet him; wait till I tell you. This is what the holes in the wall were for: they were so arranged, as to direction, that each morning, an hour after sunrise, the sun's rays would enter through one of them and shine directly on Tsianina's face. That took some mathematics and some engineering. Carew had experts for that."

"Wait a minute." Cramer had an eye cocked and his cigar tilted up. "Seems to me I've heard of that stunt before."

"Maybe. The Egyptians did it in the Great Pyramid, but only for one day in the year. Carew saw 'em and raised 'em. In a basement beneath the tomb is an enormous electric motor. Every day, at noon, the platform holding the casket, and the stone steps, slide automatically to the proper position for the next morning."

The inspector grunted. "He went to a lot of trouble."

"He did. But as I say, Tsianina's people were sun worshipers, and he worshiped Tsianina, and he was a superstitious gambler. All that arrangement had a purpose. Undoubtedly you could call him a nut if he hadn't piled up more millions than he had fingers and toes; you can anyway, if you want to, but it won't have any effect on your bank account. As for the purpose of the sunshine on Tsianina's face, he made no secret of it. He often went to the tomb at daybreak and stayed there until an hour after sunrise, and when he had any sort of important decision to make, he let her make it. If at that moment the sun's rays were on Tsianina's face, it meant that he was supposed to be concentrating on his memory of her and that nothing else mattered, and therefore it was thumbs down on whatever course or action he might be contemplating; but if her face remained in shadow he was supposed to go ahead with whatever he had in mind."

"For God's sake." Cramer sounded disgusted. "I still think he went to a lot of trouble. Who kept him from fudging?"

The district attorney shook his head. "You're not a mystic, Cramer. Neither am I. I don't know whether Val Carew fudged or not, but I do know that plenty of modern buildings, right here in this modern metropolis, omit the thirteenth floor. I'm just letting you know what that tomb is like and how it got that way. You have to know, because it was in Tsianina's tomb that Val Carew was found murdered at 7:20 in the morning of Wednesday, July 7th, four weeks ago yesterday."

"Hunh. Four days after I left." Cramer took out a fresh cigar and settled into his chair. "Go ahead."

Skinner settled too. "His body was found at the foot of the stone steps leading to the platform on which the casket with Tsianina rested, huddled as if it had fallen down the steps. You'll see the photographs. A few feet away on the floor was one of the relics from the wall, an Indian war club—a round heavy stone with a hickory sapling for a handle. Carew had been struck twice with it—a glancing blow on the right cheekbone, and a crusher back of the left temple. The second blow caved his skull in. Also near by on the floor was another relic, an old hunting knife with a curving blade. It had been used to remove a circle of hide and hair from the top of Carew's head, some three inches in diameter. In other words, he had been scalped. The scalp was found. Among the relics on the wall is a buckskin tunic that was once worn by Tsianina's great-grandfather, and the scalp had been tucked into the girdle of that."

Cramer grunted. "This ain't a case for a detective inspector, what you need is Buffalo Bill. Who found the body, a party of Boy Scouts?"

"No. Woodrow Wilson."

"Who?" Cramer stared. He growled sarcastically, "I see you're being funny. I'm still sore and I'm not laughing. Save the gags till next time."

"It wasn't a gag. Carew's body was found by Woodrow Wilson. When Carew came east in 1913 with his wife and young son, and his stake, an Indian came along—a cousin or something of Tsianina's. The Indian decided that since he was coming to the white man's big city he should take a white man's name, and he had often heard of Woodrow Wilson because Wilson was President then, so he picked that one. I suppose it doesn't matter what his Indian name was, and it's a good thing it doesn't, because he claims he has forgotten it. I don't know how old he was in 1913, but now he appears to be somewhere between sixty and ninety. He grunts exactly the way an Indian is supposed to grunt. For the past ten years, since Tsianina died, he has spent most of his time hanging around her tomb, either inside or outside the high yew hedge which surrounds it. He was doing that on the morning of July 7th, having left the house before daybreak, and he saw Carew enter the tomb, letting himself in with his key for the triple Willentz lock. Sunrise that morning was at 4:30—5:30 daylight saving; so Carew would have been awaiting the sun on Tsianina's face, if any, at half past six. The Indian says that he and Carew spoke to each other. Only three people besides Carew were ever permitted to enter the tomb: Woodrow Wilson, Amory Buysse of the National Indian Museum, and Guy Carew, the son. But the Indian says he didn't enter that morning. About forty minutes after sunrise, which would have been at 6:10, he was standing by a gap at the end of an alley in the yew hedge, when something hit him from behind. That's all he knows about it, or all he'll tell; he was knocked out. He had a bruise on his scalp. When he came to he was tied and gagged with strips of his own shirt. He worked himself loose and went to the tomb and found Carew's body there. He says he touched nothing and went to the house almost immediately, and he got to Guy Carew's room a minute or two before 7:30."

Cramer interrupted chewing his cigar to mutter half to himself, "More than four weeks ago. I hate these damned stale setups. When did we first get it?"

"Well, we haven't got it. We have and we haven't. It wasn't in our county and it still isn't our case, but Anderson of Westchester started yelling uncle two weeks ago, and of course we have to co-operate, and besides, most of the investigation has centered in New York. Carew lived at Lucky Hills only four months of the year. The newspapers and the public regard it as a New York case, and we can't laugh that off. You'll have to take it, that's all there is to it, and give it all you've got. I've given you the bare facts, and now you'd better go through the reports and all this stuff, then see the commissioner and me again, and then have a talk with Anderson. As you say, it's stale, so you can't rush anyone off his feet anyhow."

"Yeah." The inspector sounded sour and doubtful. "I'd like to ask, are any of you playing a favorite?"

Police Commissioner Humbert put in abruptly, "The Indian did it."

"You mean Woodrow Wilson?"

"I do."

"Motive?"

"You'll get it in the reports. Carew was about to forsake the memory of Tsianina and get married again."

"Okay." Cramer turned back to the district attorney. "Okay?"

"No. I doubt it." Skinner hesitated. "It's a damned complicated case. Anderson had the Indian in jail for two weeks and then turned him loose when Guy Carew got Sam Orlik on the job. There's no good line anywhere."

Cramer regarded him, and after a moment said slowly, "I wish to admit one thing. I said I knew nothing about it, but the truth is that on the train today I got into a little discussion with fellow passengers, just as a citizen. I heard a lot of scandal, nothing to it of course, but has anybody showed an inclination to try putting Guy Carew in jail?"

A swift glance passed between the two officials. Cramer grinned and continued, "Let me tell you. Once upon a time, long before there were any Indians around Mount Kisco, a fellow had his throat cut and died. When an honest detective found out who did it, it turned out to be a philanthropist named Izzy Gazooks, who owned both banks of the Hudson River and was vice-president of the Society for the Prevention of Cruelty to Politicians. So the detective moved to the country and kept chickens. Well, I suppose it is understood that I don't like chickens?"

The police commissioner spluttered, "You're crazy. We wouldn't have hauled you back from Canada if what we were looking for was a cover."

"Good. Then Guy Carew is just folks?"

"He is," Skinner snapped. "And since you've put it that way, I may as well tell you that I think Anderson fumbled on him. Guy Carew is half Indian. Tsianina was his mother, and his father was about to marry again. Guy inherits the entire fortune. His father had for years furnished him large sums for the work he was doing among the Indians, and Guy had learned that that generosity was likely to be stopped. Guy had just returned from the West and was there on July 7th, in the house at Lucky Hills. I would have advised Anderson to charge him two weeks ago but for one thing, his alibi."

"Oh. Good one?"

"Well. A woman was in his room with him from 2:00 A.M. until the Indian arrived to report the murder."

"A good woman? I mean good for credibility?"

"I would say yes. Portia Tritt."

"Don't know her. Do you?"

"I had met her. Handsome and smart. She had hooked old Carew. He was going to marry her."

Cramer grunted. "And she was in Guy's room from 2:00 A.M. on. Nice picture. Is Guy a roving stag?"

"Not by reputation. There was something years ago with Portia Tritt—you'll read it here. Since the murder he has seen a lot of her. Then recently he took up with another one, another smart one, a gal by the name of Jean Farris, a designer. It's all in the reports. Of course we're on him all the time, and for the past week we've had a tail on this Jean Farris too; the case has got to the point where you could call it desperate. Portia Tritt's alibi for Guy Carew may be a phoney, but try and prove it, or even guess why it should be. Besides those two, there were four guests at Lucky Hills that night: Leo Kranz, textile importer, an old friend of Carew's; Amory Buysse, curator of the National Indian Museum, which Carew had endowed and was supporting; and Melville Barth and his wife, of Barth & Pomeroy, Wall Street and railroads. But it's quite possible that they're all innocent; anyone who knew the place and knew Carew's habits could easily have got into the grounds and to the tomb without being seen—except by the Indian, and he was knocked cold. So he says."

"Nothing left for the sweepers?"

"Damn little. Just two things, and Anderson claims that first-rate men did the job. Fingerprints of Portia Tritt were found in four places: on the brass door of the tomb and its lever handle, on one of the relic cabinets—not the one where the knife had been—on the glass top of Tsianina's casket, and on the handle of a lance. The lance was hanging in its proper place on the wall, and its iron head showed no sign of recent use. Portia Tritt says that Carew had taken her there a week before his death."

"I thought only the son and Buysse and the Indian were allowed to enter."

Skinner shrugged. "That's her story. There were no prints on the knife or the war club. The other thing Anderson's men found was a clue that seemingly should lead to the answer, and maybe it should but it hasn't. Clutched tight in the fingers of Carew's left hand was a piece of thread—or yarn or whatever you want to call it. It was wool, dark red, an inch and a half long. The bets are on the probability that when he got the glancing blow on the cheek Carew grabbed for the intruder and pulled that piece of thread from his clothes, and the next blow smashed his head in. So you'd think with modern laboratory methods that thread would lead to the answer; and to some extent it has. It has been identified as a piece of the yarn that Indians in the Southwest used two or three centuries ago. They called it bayeta. While he was trying to trace it Anderson kept mum about it, not wanting to tip the murderer off that he had it, but he got nowhere, and last week we decided to turn it loose in certain quarters but not to publish it. That was a mistake. We didn't find out anything, and day before yesterday it got to a reporter somehow and he made the rounds with it. We had to bear down hard to prevent publication, but the damn reporter had already done plenty of harm. He spilled it—but here." The district attorney returned the batch of papers to the folder and shoved it across. "You'll read the reports on it."

Cramer sighed, lumbered to his feet, reached for the folder and tucked it under his arm. "I guess I will," he growled. "I had an Indian guide up in Canada. I'd like to catch the dirty pup that swung that war club and ruined my vacation. Hell, I will—with that swell clue you've got, you might say his life is hanging by a thread. Ha ha ha."

He stamped out.

III

How did it happen that the press showing of Bernetta's fall line (sports, town informal, travel) was held at the elaborate country place of Mr. and Mrs. Melville Barth near Portchester, with cocktails under the trees from five till seven thirty? Such a puzzle was no puzzle to the initiated, who knew that Bernetta's real name was Ivy, that she was a first cousin of Mrs. Barth, and that Mrs. Barth had sunk $60,-000 of her husband's money in the Bernetta business before it had begun to pay. It was worth a few hours' time, a few dozen cocktails, and a little wear and tear on the grass, to help keep it paying.

Not that Mrs. Barth was ashamed of the connection or tried any camouflage. For instance, at six o'clock that afternoon, she was saying to Jean Farris, "Yes, thank goodness, it's better than ever. Everyone is here except the *Herald Tribune,* Ivy says, and I understand she's peeling, got it at Southampton last week, the sun there can be *very* bad. They are all raving about the sports ensembles Ivy made from your things—such fabrics! I tell Ivy she should have priced them at three hundred at least, but she likes volume. At two fifty she might as well be giving them away. And speaking of ensembles, I *never* saw anything like the stuff you're wearing! Did Ivy make it?"

"No. Krone."

Mrs. Barth nodded. "I thought so. His jackets always sag on the right. But *such* material! Your own, of course. The placing of that stripe is sheer genius. And the stripe itself is incredible! I never saw such a color. Unique! Ivy was telling me the other day that you pick up yarns in the most out-of-the-way places, that you even go to secondhand stores. . . ."

Jean, finishing her cocktail, made a pretense of listening. She was bored and a little irritated, but not really in a bad humor, for Ivy-Bernetta had made intelligent use of her designs on the whole and the praise had been even handsomer than usual. She let Mrs. Barth rattle on, and looked around. There were perhaps a hundred women, and half as many men, scattered around that corner of the shady lawn. White-jacketed servants moved among them with trays; one wheeled a serving wagon. In front of the main group two professionally lovely models, wearing tailored woolen dresses, paraded and smiled; and as they disappeared into a gaily colored tent, two others emerged in slacks and long flaring jackets. A genteel murmur floated over the lawn and up among the leaves; certain individuals could be seen scribbling on pads of paper, glancing up at the models, and scribbling again. Those, all women, were the elite and exclusive source of the river of publicity in American feminine fashions. The presence of three press photographers with their cameras testified that an Ivy-Bernetta showing was an event.

Some of the men looked as if they belonged there; others looked silly. One of them, middle-aged and above middle size, with black eyes and an arc of his tanned pate showing, detached himself from a group and approached Mrs. Barth with a bow.

His voice was pleasant: "I'm sure you hadn't noticed, but I haven't paid my respects. You were surrounded, as usual, when I came in. This is very nice—" he waved a hand— "very successful, I congratulate you. . . . I must congratulate you also, Miss Farris. When I first saw your things, four years ago, I told myself, 'Here is a little girl who got hold of a clever idea in Vienna; it will last a season, or possibly two.' But how wrong I was! You get better all the time. Those things here today—marvelous! A quiet assurance to their beauty—no freakishness! The sort of thing that lasts and grows. You are going to bankrupt us importers."

Jean laughed. "Don't turn my head, Mr. Kranz. Thank you for the kind words. What did you bring in last year, a million yards?"

Leo Kranz grimaced at her. "Not half of that. God be praised, I'm old and bald and I got my share before you appeared on the scene. As a matter of fact, I'm letting down on textiles and spending most of my time at my art gallery. But textiles are my first love." He faked sudden anxiety. "You don't paint in oils, do you?"

"Nope. I sell by the yard only."

"Well, that's a relief—I tell you, Mrs. Barth, this girl's a menace to the trade. Whereas you are only a menace to happiness. My resp—I *am* sorry!"

Backing for a bow, he had stepped on an approaching foot. Its owner, one of the white-jacketed servants, pardoned him and circled to address Mrs. Barth:

"Two men to see you, madam. They were told you are engaged, but they insisted. Mr. Beesy, who has called twice when you were out. There is an individual with him."

"Beesy?" Mrs. Barth was frowning. "What does he— Oh. I know." The frown deepened. "That old nuisance. Why didn't you—" She stopped. "Where is he?"

"On the east terrace, madam."

"Well, tell him—" She stopped again, and looked helpless. "He'll sit there all day and all night. Will you please ask Mr. Barth to come here? He's over there by the horse chestnut—no, that one."

The servant went. Mrs. Barth sighed and turned to Jean: "I suppose you know I was at Lucky Hills, with my husband, the night Val Carew was murdered. Mr. Kranz was too." She shivered a little. "It still affects my stomach to speak of it, I suppose because the news of it came before breakfast. My stomach isn't much before breakfast. And all the questions and the publicity, and this man keeps coming, though there isn't a blessed thing I can tell him—"

She broke off at the approach of a lean little man with a leathery skin, gray hair, and chilly blue eyes. But she waited until he was close to speak: "Mel dear, did Ferguson tell you? That man Buysse is here again. He asked for me and he's on the east terrace. There's someone with him."

The eyes of most men grow either warmer or colder as they regard their wives, but Melville Barth's did neither; they merely retained their chill. He inquired quietly, "Who is with him?"

"I don't know. Ferguson said, an individual."

"Well? See him and get rid of him."

"But I don't want to. I don't want to talk about it. You know very well what I thought of going to Lucky Hills at the time, and then that awful thing happened—after all, if business required it—it isn't fair that *I* should have all the unpleasantness—"

Barth's shoulders moved with the suggestion of a shrug, and he turned to where the servant discreetly waited. "Ferguson? Please. Those men are on the east terrace? Bring them here." He disregarded the beginnings of expostulation from his wife, and turned again: "How do you do, Miss Farris. You look very charming." But the eyes remained the same. "Don't go, Kranz. Stay with us, if you don't mind. Let's see what's biting this fellow Buysse; he's making a nuisance of himself. By the way, I don't believe I've seen you since that—that morning. Of course they've been hounding you too?"

Kranz nodded. "I've been asked a million questions by a dozen different people." He sent his black eyes directly into Barth's blue ones. "Naturally, I wouldn't mind the hounding as much as you. Since I was an old and close friend of Carew's, I am perfectly willing to be annoyed in the effort to find out who killed him, whereas your only connection with him was a business one . . ."

The sentence came to a halt on its way uphill. Barth smiled thinly in cold amusement. "Quite so," he agreed. "You mean, it is being said that I was summoned to Lucky Hills that night, and my wife's presence was requested as an added touch of humiliation because some years ago she snubbed Carew's Indian wife. And that I had to go because Carew had me in a hole on Western Chemical. That's what they say. Is that what you had in mind?"

"Not prominently." Kranz was unperturbed. "I only meant I am apt to be more tolerant of the hounding than you are. For you Carew's death may have been the source of serious annoyance, but for me it was personal calamity. . . ."

Jean, feeling intrusive and uncomfortable, had half arisen to go, but had been restrained by Mrs. Barth's tug at her sleeve and a vocal remonstrance which she only half heard. She was uncomfortable because she knew that these people could not be aware of her private reason for intimate and intense concern with the sensational Carew murder case; but she submitted to the tug at her sleeve without further protest because the two men talking—not to mention the woman—

had been at Lucky Hills when it happened, and a third was coming.

The third presently arrived, following the white-jacketed Ferguson, and accompanied by the individual. They were so obviously outlanders, from the standpoint of a New York fashion group, that curious glances met them as they passed the crowd. The one immediately behind Ferguson was an inch over six feet, with a square jaw and a mane of wavy gray, almost white, hair; and he had to cut his stride not to step on his guide's heels. He wore unpressed gabardine pants which were too short for him, a pink shirt, a buckskin vest with rows of brightly colored beads on it, and, in lieu of a necktie, a bandanna neckerchief which either an old cowhand or a debutante who had spent a month on a dude ranch would have called a tough rag. No coat and no hat. The individual trotting in his rear was less spectacular, but in his way fully as notable. Between sixty and ninety was as close a guess as could be made; the dark skin of his face was deeply seamed and ridged, and the cheekbones jutted up like hames; his eyes were black slits, hardly perceptible under the down-turned brim of his immaculate Panama hat; and his natty youthful Palm Beach suit, shaped at the waist, and blue linen shirt and red four-in-hand, were completely shocking when you saw his wrinkled old face.

But they were both quite self-possessed, obviously innocent of any consciousness of incongruity, as they stopped in front of Mrs. Barth. The six-footer with the tough rag sent a slow glance around from face to face and then settled on Mrs. Barth. His voice was as soft and unobtrusive as the footfall of a wildcat.

"Howdo, everybody. I just wanted to speak with you, Mrs. Barth. But these . . ." He repeated the slow glance around.

"How do you do, Mr. Buysse." It was Melville Barth's greeting, not especially warm. "If what you want to talk about is that Lucky Hills business—though I can't imagine why you should want to speak with my wife about that—won't I do? My wife doesn't like to discuss it for two reasons: she knows nothing whatever about it, and any mention of it upsets her, because it was—unpleasant."

"Yes." Buysse looked at him. "It sure was unpleasant. But I'm afraid you won't do, Mr. Barth. I'd like to have a little talk with your wife without so many folks around. I didn't know that waiter was bringing me out to a party like this, or I'd have stayed on the terrace. Maybe you'd go back there with me, ma'am? Or somewhere—"

"Nonsense." Barth was sharper. "My wife knows nothing

24

about it. Even if she did, why should she discuss it with you? After all, Mr. Buysse, you were merely there, in the house—as we all were."

The six-footer nodded. "Sure, I was there. You mean I was just one of the bunch and the police are as interested in me as in any of you." His square jaw tightened all but imperceptibly, then relaxed again, and there was no change in his soft voice. "I know all that. I may be no different to the law, but to myself I'm plenty different. I don't want to bore you folks, but I wonder if you all know that I was a friend of Val Carew's more than thirty years ago out West? I didn't have either his luck or his brains. I used to paint pictures of Indians, but they were rotten pictures. In 1920, when Val decided to use a million out of his pile for setting up an Indian museum, he went to a lot of trouble to look me up and put me in charge of it. If it hadn't been for Val Carew, do you know what I'd be doing now? Neither do I. Anyhow I set to work, and people like Bella Weitzner consider me an authority on Indian cultures in all areas except the caribou and guanaco, and if you don't think Val and I made a good museum, go and take a look at it. So as I say, where anything connected with Val Carew is concerned, in his life or in his death, I consider myself plenty different from anyone else in these parts. And a month has gone by since he was murdered—four weeks yesterday—and if anybody has noticed the dirty coyote who did it having a trap sprung on him would they please point it out to me. That's why I think a little action won't hurt, and that's why I regard it as a proper step for me to request a little talk with Mrs. Barth."

Leo Kranz looked alert and interested, but skeptical. Jean Farris was staring fascinated at the combination of the bandanna tough rag and the beadwork on the buckskin vest. Mrs. Barth sat with her lips compressed and her gaze directed at her husband.

Her husband appeared unimpressed. He repeated impatiently, "Nonsense. I tell you she knows nothing about it. What the devil do you want to talk about? What can she tell you?"

Buysse looked at him. "Maybe not much." He looked at Mrs. Barth. "I'd had it in mind to ask you this a little different, ma'am, but I'm being crowded. You might even say rode off. What did you do with the peach you took from the dinner table that evening?"

Everybody looked astonished, Mrs. Barth most of all. She stared at him. "Peach? Good heavens, what peach? What are you talking about?"

"The peach you took that evening at Lucky Hills. When the fruit was brought on at the end of dinner, you said that you liked fruit just before going to bed, and Val said he would have some peaches sent to your room, and you said he needn't bother, you had to go up for something anyway, and you picked a peach from the bowl and took it with you. We all saw you do it."

"Well, I didn't steal it, did I?"

"No. But if you don't mind I'd like to know, what did you do with it?"

Mrs. Barth shrugged. "I suppose I ate it. Really, Mr. Buysse, I don't seriously doubt your sanity—" She stopped, and appeared to decide the thing was amusing. "Now let's see, I should be able to remember that peach, I'm very fond of them—I'm sure I ate it—of course I did! I remember biting into it—"

She stopped again, abruptly, and everyone saw the quick change on her face. Obviously, suddenly she did remember, and the memory held something both unwelcome and embarrassing. She tried to stammer out of it: "It—the peach—I remember it was very good but not quite ripe enough—it was a clingstone, you know—"

Her husband demanded, "What the devil is this nonsense, anyway?"

Buysse, disregarding him, shook his head at Mrs. Barth. "Understand, ma'am, I don't want to make trouble for someone who hasn't already made some for themselves. I'll tell you how this happened. There were no outdoor peaches ripe at Lucky Hills in early July. Those peaches on the table were expensive, big clings grown under glass. Nobody else carried one from the table. I've asked Orson, the butler, about it, and he's sure that none were served to anyone except at the table, and that none of the servants took any. He's particular with the fancy stuff. The reason I asked Orson was that a little after sunrise on July 7th, the morning after that dinner and the morning Val was murdered, a seed from one of those peaches was found on the grass inside the yew hedge which surrounds Tsianina's tomb."

A silence. It was broken by Leo Kranz. He inquired politely, "Who found it?"

"I found it."

Their stares were startled to a new focus. It was more like a dry rattle from a mummy than a living voice, and it came from the wrinkled old face beneath the immaculate Panama hat.

"Ah!" Kranz said. "Of course."

Barth demanded, "Who are you?"

"Me?" The dry dead rattle. "Woodrow Wilson."

Jean Farris sternly controlled a strong impulse to giggle. As an incident possibly relevant to tragedy, Woodrow Wilson finding a peach seed on the grass near the tomb of an Indian princess was beyond the bounds of solemnity. But unquestionably everyone was solemn; she controlled the impulse.

Buysse was saying, "Wilson has been the guardian of Tsianina's tomb for ten years, since her death. He is there every morning at daybreak. When he found the seed it was fresh; the shreds clinging to it were moist. It is true there was dew. I don't see how anybody can deny it was the seed of the peach taken by Mrs. Barth. Without any apologies, what I want to know is, who put it there and when."

Barth snapped, "Rot. There's not the slightest proof it was that peach, and what if it was? Carew was alive at sunrise."

"I still want to know."

Mrs. Barth had sat with compressed lips. Now she spoke, exasperated. "All right, I'll tell you. As I said, I ate the peach—"

"Be quiet, Laura." The husband taking command. "This man has no right whatever to demand explanations, even if there were anything to explain. He's butting in, and he can butt out again."

"Sure I can." Buysse was patient. "I only intimated it seems to me the police are doing a dog dance, and if they're too busy on that to start a trail, maybe someone else can. Maybe me, for instance. But if I can't even get an answer to a little question about a peach seed, I'm licked, and all I can do is turn the seed over to the police—I've got it here in my pocket—and let them use it in their dance."

Leo Kranz had brows raised at him. "In a way, it really belongs to the police, doesn't it?"

"I'm not worried about who it belongs to. What I want to know is how it got there. That's what they'll want to know too."

"I expect they will." Kranz's voice was as soft as the other's. "But you seem to have restrained your curiosity—for a whole month?"

"No. Wilson only told me about it three days ago. I've been trying to see Mrs. Barth."

"Then Wilson restrained his curiosity. I've often heard Val say that no one has more than an Indian. How about it, Wilson?"

The Panama hat moved slowly to one side and back again. The dry rattle sounded: "Too many words."

"Oh, no, Wilson. You forget that I know you. You know what curiosity means as well as I do. Why did you wait nearly four weeks to tell about the peach seed?" Kranz took a quick step and stooped a little to get his gaze under the brim of the Panama. "Look here," he demanded sharply. "Did you eat that peach yourself?"

"Me?" The old Indian grunted. "I always said you are a damn fool."

Kranz started to demand again, but was interrupted. "This is perfectly idiotic!" Mrs. Barth's exasperation was obviously mounting. "Didn't I say I ate the peach? And I ate it—no, Mel, you be quiet yourself! Mr. Buysse is right; he'll turn that silly seed over to the police, and for heaven's sake, haven't you had enough of *that*? Let me alone." She addressed Buysse: "Since you seem to have so good a memory of that evening, you probably remember that after dinner my husband went to the library with Mr. Carew and I went upstairs. I stayed there a while and then came down again, and left the house by the doors at the end of the corridor where the tapestries are—I don't know what you call it—"

Buysse nodded. "The north wing. How did you happen to go that way?"

She compressed her lips at him. "I went that way because I didn't care to meet anyone, and I didn't care to meet anyone because I was going to see that tomb which of course was notorious, and I didn't regard it as anybody's business. Indians aren't the *only* curious people in the world, and I knew the way from the discussion at dinner, though I wasn't going to admit I would care to look at the thing. It was a nice starlit night, and I found it easily. I went inside the yew hedge and walked all around it. It happens that in addition to being curious I like to eat fruit outdoors when I am alone because it doesn't matter how the juice drips, and I took the peach along and ate it there, and naturally I dropped the seed on the ground. I suppose I would have dug a hole and buried it if I had known it was going to be regarded as a *clue*." She sighed. "Really, of all the insane—"

Buysse had his eyes straight at hers. "So you ate the peach there Tuesday night. Not Wednesday morning."

"I've answered your question, Mr. Buysse."

"I know you have, ma'am, much obliged. And what I really had in mind, you ate it yourself. You understand, I didn't really have any idea—what do you want?"

That was not for Mrs. Barth. What had interrupted him

was a tug at his sleeve from the rear, from Woodrow Wilson. Apparently what the old Indian wanted was gangway, for, disregarding Buysse's question, he made his way past him to the inside of the circle, crossed so close to Mrs. Barth that she shrank involuntarily, and stopped in front of Jean Farris, within a foot of her, peering intently. But seemingly it wasn't Jean's face that interested him, for his gaze was aimed at a point on her jacket halfway between her chin and her waist.

Leo Kranz demanded, "What are you doing? What do you want?"

"Me?" Nothing of the Indian moved but his lips, and they scarcely visibly. "I like to touch."

"Touch what? You ought to know better—"

But Jean understood, or thought she did. The dark old wrinkled face so close to her was a little disconcerting, but she smiled at it and assured it, "Go ahead. I don't mind."

He put out a hand, in no haste, slipped two fingers under the edge of the jacket at the spot where the red stripe began, and rubbed the material, slowly and delicately, between his thumb and fingers. Then he leaned over to peer more closely, and rubbed some more.

He grunted, straightened up, and stepped back. Jean spoke: "You are perfectly correct, Mr. Wilson. You have good eyes."

"For heaven's sake," Mrs. Barth exclaimed, "what is it he's correct about?"

She got no answer because of a new interruption. They had all been too intent on the Indian's tableau to notice the couple's approach, and were aware of them only when the voice sounded from behind Leo Kranz:

"He'll never tell you, Mrs. Barth! Not *that* Indian! I know him. How do you do? I'm afraid we're a little late—but the traffic!"

She came through a gap in the circle—rather tall, moderately slender under a blue summer-weight mantle, not one of the youngsters but by no means in need of generosity from them, with fair skin untanned but not pallid, alert gray eyes, and soft light hair, neither brown nor yellow, showing at one edge of an elegantly tricky little hat. She paired well, by contrast, with the man behind her—dark but not swarthy, around thirty, tall, with the breadth of an athlete, a sober face if not solemn, black eyes that were certainly more than slits and still might somehow vaguely remind you of the eyes that had been peering at the stripe in Jean Farris's jacket.

There were greetings and handshakings, expressions of astonishment by the man at finding Buysse and the old

Indian there and an appearance of embarrassment as his hand met the hand of Melville Barth, a sudden artificial gaiety on the part of Jean Farris—surprising since not even malice had ever called her artificial—and a darting of the eyes of Leo Kranz, apparently not to miss any movement or gesture of the woman in the tricky little hat.

The woman was speaking to Mrs. Barth: "Oh, yes, we've been here a quarter of an hour or more—over at the other side of the crowd—I suppose you couldn't see us. Extremely successful, really! I can see a headline: *Bargains in Beauty by Bernetta!* I shall certainly advise Beecher to take at least eight numbers—and I want Renée of Hollywood to see them—"

"That's very nice of you." Mrs. Barth looked pleased. "Ivy was saying to me yesterday, 'No one is as important as Portia Tritt. If Portia Tritt likes them—' "

Portia Tritt laughed. "I'd love to think that, but I'm afraid Ivy exaggerates. I do know how to put a thing over, though, and it's always a relief to find something that's worth the trouble aside from the pay one gets for it. To be perfectly frank, I think Ivy owes a lot to those Jean Farris fabrics." She turned. "They're the best you've done yet, Jean. They'll certainly put you at the top if you're not there already. That cashmere check in brick and blue with the repeats diminishing on both sides of the seam—good heavens! Stand up!"

Jean obediently stood up. Portia Tritt gazed. "Turn around. Ah, I see! Back to the other side—do you mind? Did Bernetta make it?"

"No, Krone."

"Then you designed it. Probably you cut it yourself. I wish I had your hands. The way you swing that stripe across is almost *too* clever. You're a subtle girl, Jean. And the stripe itself—what is it? I've never seen such a red. Look, Guy! Leo! That stripe. Did you ever see such a color as that?"

Guy Carew's black eyes surveyed the jacket, Jean's face, and the face of Portia Tritt. He shook his head faintly and said nothing. Leo Kranz, omitting Jean's face, said, "It's remarkable. I had noticed it before you came."

Mrs. Barth put in, "I'd like to know why that Indian stared at it and felt it and Miss Farris said he was correct. Correct about what?"

"It's no mystery," Jean said. "I use mostly modern yarn, of course, but I get old yarn from lots of places, anywhere I can. There are many old yarns that couldn't possibly be duplicated today." She touched the stripe. "This is genuine bayeta."

"What's that?"

"An old Spanish yarn. In the sixteenth and seventeenth centuries they made a red vegetable dye in Persia, and sold it to Spain. The Spaniards dyed yarn with it and made soldiers' pants from the material they wove with the yarn. The soldiers wore the pants to America and had them on when they were fighting the Indians, and got killed. The Indians took the pants and unraveled them, and used the yarn in weaving their finest blankets. The blankets are still called bayeta—those with some of that yarn in them—and most of the best ones are in museums. If you get hold of one that's damaged, or a piece of one, of course, you can unravel it again and use the yarn."

"May I?" Mrs. Barth reached across to finger the stripe. "Do you mean to say that's three hundred years old?"

"Two or three hundred."

"And it holds that color! And it was part of a soldier's pants! And that—Mr. Wilson recognized it." She looked at the old Indian with an interest slightly apprehensive. "It almost makes you feel he might have killed the soldier."

Guy Carew smiled. "Wilson's not quite that old, Mrs. Barth, and besides, he's a Cherokee. Cherokees never got a crack at Spanish soldiers; that was in the Southwest."

"Then how did he recognize it?"

"Oh, I suppose—" Guy turned. "How did you recognize it, Wilson? From the museum blankests?"

"Me?" The Indian grunted. "To hell with it. Too many words."

Portia Tritt inquired, "But, Jean, where on earth did you get the yarn?"

"Oh . . ." Jean faintly flushed, and fluttered a hand. Then she met Portia Tritt's eye and said abruptly, "Mr. Carew gave it to me."

"I see." Portia Tritt's brows went up. "Generous of you, Guy." She smiled at Jean. "Would you mind having a twin? Have you any more of it?"

"Not an ounce."

Leo Kranz observed, "Of course that sort of thing isn't in trade, not really. It's too rare, even for Fifty-seventh Street. And speaking of trade—if the rest of you don't mind—could you come to the gallery tomorrow, Portia? I think I know a new channel for some Lamois publicity. . . ."

The group began to disintegrate. Leo Kranz and Portia Tritt drew aside. Guy Carew got into conversation with Buysse and the Indian. Jean Farris was carried off toward the gaily colored tent by two women with pencils and pads in their hands. Mrs. Barth started briskly in the direction of the main crowd, probably to learn at firsthand from Ivy how things were going; but before she reached the fringe she was halted by the sound of her husband's voice calling her name. She turned and waited for him to come up.

"It occurred to me, Laura—" Mr. Barth glanced around; there was no one in hearing distance of a low-pitched voice. "I understand some of these people are staying to dinner."

His wife responded quickly to the irritation in his tone and on his face. "Yes, and you promised to be here. Good lord, it's only once a year, and only a couple of hours—"

"I know, I know. I can stand it. Who will be here?"

"Oh, that Desher woman from the *Times,* and two from *Harvey's Bazaar,* and that man from London, and—Miss Graham has the list. Portia Tritt. Apparently she brought Guy Carew with her, so I can ask him if you think I should—"

"By all means."

"All right, I'll ask him. I've told Grimm dinner at nine, on the terrace, informal of course, since they'll just stay on and brought nothing with them. Oh, yes, I asked Jean Farris. And I suppose I might as well include Mr. Kranz; that might be amusing when you consider Portia Tritt."

Her husband nodded. "I'm glad you can be amused. I wanted to suggest that you invite that fellow Buysse and the Indian."

Mrs. Barth stared. "Good heavens, why?"

"Because I suggest it." He glanced around again. "I've told you, haven't I, that Val Carew's death didn't remove my difficulties? It merely forces me to deal with the son and heir instead. You saw how he greeted those two. I think it might make a good impression on him if we have them at the dinner table. Little things like that make a big difference sometimes."

"Well." Mrs. Barth sighed. "This fashion bunch may be peculiar in some respects, but at least they're not Indians. I might as well start a circus."

"Nonsense." He was crisp. "Will you ask them?"

"Yes."

"So they'll accept?"

"Yes. You don't need to pour acid on me." She frowned. "Look here, Mel, is this thing no better? Is it as bad as ever?" She suddenly raised her voice: "I had no idea there would be so many—no, indeed, Miss Desher, you're not interrupting at all—I believe you've met my husband—"

Guy Carew was saying to Amory Buysse, "I'm aware that I have no right to give you orders, but I asked you not to.

Didn't I? And I find you here asking God knows what. If you thought that peach seed meant anything, you should have turned it over to the police. Didn't I tell you that?"

"Sure you did." Buysse slowly shook his head. "No, Guy, I don't believe it would do any good no matter what you turned over to the police. In a general sort of way you can give me orders because you're your father's son, but on a trail you don't know it's better to give me my head. I've seen more badger holes than you have. Hell, you're just a kid."

"My God, I'm thirty-one years old. I'm not letting anyone feed me rabbit stew. I've dealt with Indian agents and concession hounds and cattlemen who don't like any fences except their own—and anyway, he was my father."

The old Indian, his head tilted back a little to peer at the taller men from under the brim of his Panama, grunted. "That girl," he said. "What did she feed you? You're not a kid. You're a man."

"She didn't feed me anything. What do you mean, Wilson?"

The Indian grunted again. "You saw me feel it."

"I know I did. What do you know about it?"

"Me? Nothing."

"The devil—" Guy Carew shrugged. "I can't get it out of you here. But I will." He shifted to Buysse. "And you too. I'm damn tired of all this silent paddle stuff. Of course you know the police are following all of us everywhere we go. I'll see you tonight, you and Wilson both. . . ."

Buysse and the Indian, both motionless, stood and listened.

Leo Kranz, toward the end of his conversation with Portia Tritt, employed a phrase nearly identical with one Guy had used to Buysse. He said, "I can't finish it here. I think Ella Desher is headed for you now. But it won't do, Portia." His voice was tense, his eyes level into hers. "I tell you it won't do."

"I don't say it will." Her smile proclaimed no amusement. "But who says it won't?"

"I do. I've been patient; I always am. No one knows that better than you. But your bringing him here today—under all the circumstances—"

"My dear Leo!" She laughed with light assurance. "I told you long ago I won't stand for a bridle, let alone spurs. And you know very well I have never given you the slightest— Oh, hello, Ella! No, really, I was just telling Mr. Kranz that I hoped you wouldn't be completely overwhelmed—"

It was after eight o'clock when Jean Farris finally escaped

from the admiring clutches of a pair of persistent ladies who wanted to write her up for a magazine still in the period of gestation which was to be called *The Covered Woman*. They were the last of the cocktail guests to go. The dinner guests were scattered around the grounds, or in the house; on that portion of the lawn Jean was alone except for two men in white jackets who were stacking folding chairs in piles and raking up rubbish. She stood with her back pressed against the trunk of a maple tree, with her arms up for her hands to clasp on top of her head, and her eyes closed. She felt tired and not at all gay, and was wishing that she had either drunk more cocktails or had refused the two she had taken.

"Oh, there you are!"

Jean gave a little start and opened her eyes. She didn't feel like smiling at the man who was striding towards her, so she didn't try to.

She said, "You walk differently, you really do. As if your toes had more to do with it—but still not exactly like the Indians I've seen in New Mexico."

"Well, I'm not from New Mexico." Guy Carew stood and looked down at her. "You look different too, the way you were standing against that tree. Who were you posing for?"

She shook her head. "I was just resting. A tree does rest me that way. Maybe I'm a half-breed dryad. What are you wandering around for?"

"I was looking for you."

"Here I am."

"So I see." He came a step closer. "I want to ask you something. As you observed the other day, I don't know how to use finesse. I'm too direct, but I can't help it. Will you give me that—those things you're wearing? That skirt and jacket?"

"Give you—" She stared. "You mean *give* them to you?"

"Yes. I can't say lend, because I don't know . . . You can imagine how I hate to ask you, but that's what I mean. Give them to me. And I can't explain, at least not satisfactorily. I can only say that something has happened which makes it very desirable that I have them."

Jean looked at him. Finally she said quietly, "I begin to understand why some people are called Indian givers. I had always supposed it was slander."

"It is. It's a detestable phrase. If I could only—"

Jean's sudden burst of laughter stopped him. "Excuse me," she cried, "but it's funny! Very funny! Less than an hour ago Mr. Barth hunted me up to tell me that his wife was crazy about it and he would like to buy it for her—of course, he said, knowing its history, he would expect to pay a stiff price for it, but he would expect me to authenticate the bayeta yarn—and now you want me to give it back to you—" Jean laughed again. Then she sobered, and continued in a tone of great friendliness, "It shows you have good judgment, anyway. Portia Tritt would look very nice in it."

"Portia! Good lord—wait a minute!"

But Jean, who could move swiftly on occasion, kept going. She tossed back over her shoulder, "She would look nice in it, but she can't have it!"

She was twenty paces off when Guy, moving more swiftly still, overtook her, gripped her arm, and stopped her. She whirled to face him, and there was bite in her voice:

"Mr. Carew! Really!"

He released her arm, and stood. She moved again, off across the lawn—hearing his footsteps after her again—no, that was something else—he wasn't coming—yes, he was —no—

No.

She went on, came to a graveled drive and crossed it, detoured around a bank of rhododendrons ten feet high, and went on again. There was no sound of pursuit. She became aware that she was passing the cutting garden, where the year previously she had been taken by Ivy-Bernetta to gather gladioli. She left it behind. There was another stretch of lawn, or rather mowed meadow grass, and finally a thicket of mixed shrubbery beyond which she caught a glimpse of the fence which bounded the estate. Practical considerations arose. She might be able to climb the fence, but didn't care to. Her car was parked far away, in the space on the other side of the house. There was no point in racing around the boundary of the grounds. She chose a grassy spot beside a luxuriant shrub with dark-green leaves, lay down flat on her back, and closed her eyes.

She was furious; she had made a howling fool of herself. It was no mitigation that she could list the contributing causes; still she listed them. First chronologically, her moderately unpleasant surprise at the appearance of Guy Carew as the escort of Portia Tritt. Second, his stoical inattention to the presence of herself and what she was wearing. Third, the unfortunate coincidence that in the dressing tent she had heard two women discussing with gusto the affair which, according to gossip, had taken place some eight years previously, with Guy Carew and Portia Tritt as the principals. Fourth, the fact that when she had heard his voice as she stood against the tree, her heart had jumped. At that very moment she had been deciding that nothing could be sillier than her imagining she wanted a husband—and then merely at the sound of his voice her heart had jumped.

She opened her eyes, looked for five minutes past the shrubbery's edge at the sky growing dim for the evening, and closed them again. It was incredible that she had said that to him about Portia Tritt. Even if her intention to have him for a husband had been anything more than a joke, even if she had been halfway serious about it on account of some crazy impulse, it remained the sort of thing that Jean Farris would never stoop to. Even if she should again some time decide that he had desirable qualities as a—well, as a companion—which of course was out of the question and worth thinking of only as pure hypothesis—even so, she would never care to be with him again after making that exhibition of herself.

For many minutes, lying there on the grass beneath the shrub, she let that pot of self-scorn simmer within her breast, and kept stirring it and poking at it, as the dusk of twilight slowly settled onto the meadow. Once, hearing a rustling near by, she opened her eyes; but, deciding it was a scampering squirrel or rabbit and not worthy of investigation, she closed them again without turning her head.

Well . . . she had accepted Mrs. Barth's invitation to dinner. It must be nearing nine o'clock. She would have to get up, brush herself off, walk back to the house, and join the gay party. Tomorrow morning she would have the skirt and jacket packed and sent by parcel post to Guy Carew. Indian giver! Was it actually possible that he wanted them for Portia Tritt—to have her wear the bayeta? In that case, he was socially a monster . . . no, she didn't mean socially, she meant . . . to the devil with it—

The train of thought ended as if cut off by a flashing sword. What cut it was a shrill sound—a piercing, ear-splitting note—seemingly from the ground behind her head. Startled, she jerked herself up, sitting erect, and, as she did so, the sound was completed and she recognized it as the call of a whippoorwill. Simultaneously she heard a rustling of the shrub and felt something strike the side of her head. Or rather, she didn't feel, because her nervous system had quit; she was unconscious.

Twilight had thickened to darkness when she stirred. Not that she was immediately aware of it; the first twitching of her arms and legs was an experiment of the nerves, independent of the will, testing the lines of communication. Then sentience crawled timidly back and crept through the alleys of her brain. Her first demonstration of consciousness was a dim but overpowering awareness that she had a head, and cloudy irritation with it. . . . Why the deuce should so much importance be attached to anything so obvious as the fact that she had a head? Anyway, the head was no good, because it couldn't be moved—or could it? She might try— good God! It was full of hot lead! Then she remembered. She had been hit on the head, a terrific, shattering blow, by a whippoorwill. But no, it couldn't have been like that—

Hey! she jerked up sitting, terrified, in spite of the head. Something had bit her on the leg—or something sharp had stuck her— Oh. Probably a grass stubble or a twig. But by that time she was sufficiently conscious to feel astonishment that she could see her leg, both her legs, nearly all of them, quite bare from the top of her stocking to the edge of the—what was it? Shakespeares. But why, in the name of heaven, bare legs? And why—she would investigate that. With her right hand she felt at her left shoulder, and was touching thin silk. She began to realize that there was something highly peculiar about this whole situation; she had been assaulted by a whippoorwill, it was dark, and her jacket and skirt were gone. . . .

She put up her hands to feel her head.

IV

The terrace was adequately lit by two electric lanterns hanging high, surrounded at the bottom by a circular trough which was half filled with electrocuted bugs. From the table beneath the corpses could not be seen, though if you cared to look you could catch glimpses of the insects hurtling to their doom.

A fair amount of jollity was being displayed by Mr. and Mrs. Melville Barth and their twenty guests, most of which was instigated by Adele Worthy of *Harvey's Bazaar,* who told stories in a voice loud enough for all. Even Woodrow Wilson laughed heartily at her tale of the drunken Indian who operated with a hatchet on the tail of his dog because abbreviated tails were fashionable, missed his aim entirely and cut off the dog's head, and threw the hatchet down in disgust, mumbling, "Too short!" Miss Worthy regarded that tale as especially apropos for the present group, since it referred both to Indians and to fashions. She said so, and no one contradicted her.

The roast veal was being consumed, with fresh lima beans and a modest but cheerful Moselle, when the butler approached Mrs. Barth's chair and spoke unobtrusively.

"I beg your pardon, madam. Miss Graham would like to speak with you."

Mrs. Barth looked astonishment, and expressed it vocally, but the butler stuck to it that Miss Graham required the presence of her employer in the house. Forsaking remonstrance, Mrs. Barth excused herself, crossed the terrace, passed through the door held open for her, and in the large reception hall turned to confront the butler, who had followed her.

He spoke hastily, not quite his placid self: "Please, madam. It was not Miss Graham. I was following the instructions of Miss Farris. In the—er—unusual circumstances—"

"Miss Farris! What do you mean? Where is she?"

"Pardon me, madam. Her instructions were very strict. No one but you, absolutely no one, is to know of her presence, and she would like to have you come to her in the pink room on the second floor. I put her there—"

"Put her! What's wrong with her? Is she hurt?"

"No, madam. That is, not—"

He was speaking to air; Mrs. Barth was on her way. He took two steps after her, halted, hesitated, shook his head, and returned to the terrace.

Upstairs, at the door of the pink room, Mrs. Barth entered without stopping to knock. The room was lit. In a chintz-covered chair by a window sat Jean Farris, bent forward, her brow resting on both her palms. As she slowly straightened up and slowly turned her head, Mrs. Barth caught a glimpse of the garters and the bare legs. She hurried across.

"Good heavens, child! What's the matter? Where are your clothes?"

Jean said, with her head held rigid, "You asked exactly the right question. That's it."

"But what—where have you been? We couldn't imagine— we looked all over—your car was here—we decided you had gone off with someone—"

"I went off all right." Jean grimaced. "Do you mind sitting down? There, in front of me; I can't turn my head. I'm sorry to interrupt your dinner, but I didn't want to wait. ... Here's what happened—what time is it?"

"Not quite ten."

"Then I was there—but I'd better tell you. A little after eight, about a quarter after, I went for a walk. In the grounds. I crossed a drive and some more lawn and went past the cutting garden and on across the meadow until I saw the fence of the estate. I lay down on the grass by some shrubbery and closed my eyes. After a while I sat up. Just as I sat up something hit me on the side of the head and knocked me out. Here—" she gingerly touched the side of her head above the left ear— "there's a bruise and you can see the swelling. When I came to I was the way I am now. My clothes were gone."

"But—" Mrs. Barth gaped at her. "But what hit you?"

"How the dickens do I know? I didn't see anyone or hear anyone."

"But why should they take your *clothes?*"

"I don't know that either. They didn't take my watch or my ring, or my bag with money in it."

"But, my dear child—" Mrs. Barth got up and went to her and examined her head, peering at it, touching it with gentle fingers. "Knocked unconscious! You should have a doctor! How does it feel now?"

"Not very good. I don't want a doctor." Jean grimaced again, shut her lips tight, and then opened them. "I want to find who it was. That's why I interrupted your dinner. I'd like you to notify the police and get them here before any of your guests leave."

Mrs. Barth was staring at her in horror. "You don't mean —the *police!*"

"I certainly do. I've been thinking it over, as well as I can think with this head. I want—"

"But, Miss Farris! It's impossible! Think of the publicity!"

"I don't give a damn about the publicity. I don't care how ridiculous it makes me, having the clothes stolen from my back and having to ring the bell and explain my panties to your butler. Don't you realize I'm good and mad? It must have been one of the guests—who else could it be? I am *not* going to let him drive gaily home with my suit under the seat of his car, and who can stop him except the police? Of course, he may not have it. As I say, I've been trying to think. He could have bundled it up and thrown it over the fence somewhere, intending to get it later. In that case, the police should look for it. And everyone here should have to answer some questions. I'm sorry, really, but I absolutely insist . . ."

Mrs. Barth had sat down again, with the expression of one having a job to do. She made no effort to interrupt, even permitted a lengthy silence when Jean had finished, and then spoke with no heat or acrimony.

"Listen to me, Miss Farris. Won't you? I know you're a well-bred girl and wouldn't dream of making unpleasantness in another woman's house without great provocation. I don't deny you've had the provocation, but just consider. You say you're willing to incur the publicity, but what about the rest of us? We're the ones who would really get it. You're thinking about yourself, which is natural, and so you haven't stopped to realize a curious fact, that all the people who were at Lucky Hills, in Val Carew's house, the night he was murdered, are here in my house now. Guy Carew, Leo Kranz, Portia Tritt, that man Buysse and that Indian, my husband and myself. Another fact is that Val Carew was hit on the head and so were you. There's no reason to suppose there's any connection, but reason won't have much to do with it if the papers once get hold of this."

Mrs. Barth upturned both palms in desperate expostulation. "My dear, you just don't realize. It has been perfectly terrible. And if this is added to it, you being knocked on the head right here in my house, with all these people here— and the police come—it will be more than I can *bear*. They might even arrest somebody—"

Jean put in savagely, "That's exactly what I want them to do."

"In *my* house? My dear, I understand, you simply feel vindictive, and I understand that, but if you would only stop to consider—if you would just let yourself cool off a little— after all, you didn't lose anything but a suit with some old yarn in it—and I'll gladly pay you for that, whatever amount you say—"

No, Jean declared, it wasn't the money value of the suit, she didn't care about that. Then, Mrs. Barth retorted, it was pure unadulterated vindictiveness, and she had never supposed Miss Farris to be that sort of person. Mrs. Barth elaborated on that theme, developed it into an appeal to Jean's better nature, passed from that to a harrowing picture of the injury that would be done to the innocent enterprise of her cousin Ivy-Bernetta. . . .

During the latter portion of it Jean's head was resting on her hands again. Finally she said wearily, without looking up, "All right, Mrs. Barth, forget it. I've been trying to think . . . I won't insist on the police. You'll have to take my word for it that I have a particular reason for not . . . just letting it drop."

"My dear, I knew you'd be reasonable—I do hope your head—"

"Wait a minute. I'll leave the police out of it, provided you'll do something. You say all those people are here, even the Indian and Mr. Buysse?"

"Yes. I—I thought it would be only polite to ask them, since Mr. Carew—"

"All right. The point is, they're here. If you don't want the police, do exactly as I say." Jean sat up, grimaced, and held her head motionless. "Go down right now and give each of your guests a pencil and a piece of paper, and ask each one to write down what he or she was doing from 8:30 to 9:00 o'clock, without anyone discussing it with anyone else. See that they do that, and that they sign it. Then tell them—"

"But what excuse can I give for such an extraordinary—"

"I don't know. Tell them it's a game. But after you have collected the papers, not before, tell them what happened to me, just as I have told it to you. I don't want to see any of them; tell them I've gone home. Then bring—"

"But good lord! If I tell them, it will be everywhere by morning! I *can't* tell them!"

"You certainly can. Whoever did it, that's what he was counting on, that you would do everything in your power to keep it quiet. I'm offering a compromise with you, and you'd better accept it. My head hurts and I want to go home—and by the way, I'll have to beg something to wear. The truth is, Mrs. Barth, I feel utterly nasty. My head hurts, and I'm madder than I've ever been in my life, and I have special feelings that wouldn't interest you. So unless you do what I ask immediately, before anyone gets away, I'll trot downstairs in this costume and phone the police myself. The phone there on the bedstand isn't connected."

Mrs. Barth gasped. "You tried it?"

"I did. I tell you, I'm a mean customer. And did I say you are to bring the signed papers to me at once? Then I'll go. You understand, no one is to be left out—not even your husband, for instance. Also, if it isn't done just as I've said, I'm sure to hear of it—two or three good friends of mine are down there—"

"Really, Miss Farris, you have no right—"

"I know I haven't, and neither have your guests got a right to bounce a club on my head and steal my clothes. So I say it anyway, and I mean it."

Mrs. Barth got up. "Everything considered," she said stiffly, "I regard it as unfortunate that I invited you to dinner."

"We agree on that perfectly. Will you go?"

As the door closed behind her hostess, Jean slowly and carefully lowered her brow to her palms again.

Some time between eleven and midnight, towards the end of a long level stretch on the Post Road, a stern and handsome motorcycle cop leaned his vehicle against the highway railing and strode to the running board of the roadster which had pulled up at the curb in the rear, and directed his gaze at the tired-looking young woman behind the steering wheel.

"Let me see your license."

She produced it from her handbag, from which she had first to remove a thick fold of sheets of paper which had been crammed into it. He took it and examined it.

"Would you mind telling me why you're in such a hurry to get somewhere?"

She started to shake her head, then stopped with a grimace that appeared to register pain. She tried to smile at him: "I'm sorry, I can't. I promised not to notify the police."

"Oh, good at gags? You're clever?"

"I am not." She sounded weary, but emphatic. "It would be impossible to conceive of anyone as dumb as I am. You could search the world over, and in the end you would come back to me. I was probably going too fast, and I apologize. If you write out a summons, I'll take it. If you don't write out a summons, I'll dream about you."

The cop grunted. He opened his mouth, but apparently the comeback he had in mind wasn't good enough, for he abandoned it, and after another grunt turned without a word. He was just straddling his saddle when the roadster whirred by in second.

V

In the room which represented chaos, but not, as she had decided, disorder, Eileen Delaney stood at noon on Friday and, with exasperation tempered by concern, regarded her partner Jean Farris, who was removing her hat with leisurely and unprecedented gentleness. When the hat had been disposed of, on top of a pile of material which was itself piled on a box of yarn, Jean turned to say:

"I know, Eileen. I'm sorry. You're nice to be nice about it. I couldn't drag myself out of bed. I have a headache."

"What! You never have a headache."

"I know. I'm out for a record. You'd better phone Muir & Beebe and tell them a week from Monday."

"I suppose I'll have to." Miss Delaney started off, then turned back. "Did Cora tell you about your caller?"

"No, I hurried through. Who was it?"

"Not was. Is. He's out in the big room, said he'd like to see the looms going. He's been here since ten o'clock. It's your Indian."

"My—You don't mean Guy Carew?"

"Right."

"What—" Jean stared. "What does he want?"

"I didn't ask him. I presume his collar is choking him and he wants help."

Jean slowly got onto the stool, rested her elbows on the table and her forehead on her fists, and closed her eyes. After a silence she said without moving, "Send him in here. Please?"

Miss Delaney looked at her partner, opened her mouth and shut it again, and went.

When the caller entered two minutes later, Jean was quite busy. Squared paper was in front of her, a crayon in one hand and color cards in the other, and she was obviously buried in calculation. But in a couple of seconds she looked up:

"Oh, good morning. Miss Delaney tells me you've been here since ten o'clock. I'm sorry you had to wait."

"So am I." He came to the end of the table and stood, gazing at her face. "You got hurt."

"Yes. Moderately. Apparently it takes quite a blow to crack a skull open."

"I know it does. That's what happened to my father. Have you had a doctor?"

"No, I don't need one. I just have a sore head."

"That's silly." He stepped forward briskly. "There might be a minor fracture. Let me see." He had his fingers on her head before she knew what he was doing. "Which side? Oh. Not much of a bruise. Hold still."

"Stop, damn it! That hurts! Will you please let me alone?"

He stepped back, cast a glance around, went to a chair and removed from its seat various miscellaneous items, and sat down. "It's silly not to have a doctor look at it," he declared. "Why is it that some women can't be kept away from doctors, and others won't go to them at all? It seems to be universal, because Indian women are that way too."

Jean had the attitude of a person, momentarily interrupted, who expects to be immersed in her work again as soon as possible. "I don't suppose," she observed, "that you have been waiting two hours in order to establish a universal fact about women."

Guy Carew frowned, and with a deliberate forefinger rubbed the bridge of his nose. "You can imagine," he said at length, "how I have been . . . that I've been a good deal upset. I telephoned your apartment last night and got no answer. I phoned this morning and gave my name and was told that you were sleeping. I called there at 9:30 this morning and was told that you didn't feel like seeing anyone. Now that I see you . . . I told you the other day, last Saturday, that you made me think of a Kiowan phrase, 'Your eyes are open to me.' But yesterday afternoon . . . and now . . . I don't know how to say what I want to."

"Go ahead and say it. Because I'm pretty busy . . ."

His gaze was concentrated at her, his black eyes narrowed a little. "There's another saying," he declared. "This one is in Caddoan. 'When a woman grinds the corn with one hand, don't let it in your belly.' I'm not sure, but I think it means: 'Don't take a capricious woman for a wife.'"

"It seems to me," said Jean without smiling, "that you're wasting a lot of folklore. I am not capricious, and I don't *think* I've applied to anyone for a position as wife. But if I did, and you're trying to tell me that you're sorry, I can't have the job—"

"Miss Farris! Please! You know very well what I'm trying to say. I thought we were pretty good friends. If your eyes were open to me, it's quite obvious that they aren't now. I want—I needed very much to see you and ask you some things—but I can't very well ask favors of an enemy."

Jean's brows went up. "Me an enemy?"

"Certainly. Your manner and your tone of voice—you might as well be wearing a war bonnet. So that's my first question. Why?"

"Well. Since you ask it—in the first place, it seems quite possible that you hit me on the head last evening and stole my clothes."

"Me? Good God! You say I did that?"

"I said it seems possible."

"That I knocked you on the head? You aren't serious."

"I am absolutely serious."

"Then you're an awful fool." He got up, without haste, and

walked to her. He towered above her, frowning down at her, the muscles of his jaw perceptibly moving. "Look here, Miss Farris. The other day we seemed to . . . No, I won't say that. I don't know how it seemed to you. But to me it seemed—what I said, that your eyes were open to me. I felt that there was no fear and no meanness between us, and no calculation. That was the first time in my life that I ever had that feeling. I thought—from the way you talked— that you felt the same way. Perhaps I was wrong." He stopped, regarded her a moment in silence, and then returned to his chair. He repeated, this time making it a question, "Perhaps I was wrong?"

"Perhaps." Jean wasn't looking at him. As he had stood frowning down at her he had been unspeakably stern and darkly handsome, and now she wasn't looking at him. "Or perhaps I was. You really want to be frank, do you? Then for meanness, how about your asking me to give you that skirt and jacket, without any reason? Now wait a minute! It was only the second time we were together, that evening at Lucky Hills two weeks ago. When I admired that jacket you told me it was real bayeta and you'd like to have me take it. You told me it wasn't in its original blanket form anyway, and even if it had been you wouldn't care, because you'd like to see what my art could do with it. And you said—certain other things. So I took it, and I didn't even let one of my girls unravel it; I did it myself, here in this room, and I spent hours selecting yarns to go with it, and I spent twenty more hours at one of the looms, weaving it myself. Then I took it to Krone, and I wouldn't let his cutter touch it; I did the cutting. When it came yesterday I thought it was beautiful. This is what they call a sob story. When you showed up at Barth's you didn't even notice it; you barely glanced at it. That was all right; maybe you had something else to do. But a little later you calmly came and asked me to give it to you because it was desirable for you to have it!" Jean's eyes flashed at him. "I'll tell you one thing, Mr. Carew, I'm a well-known designer, and where my work is concerned I'm conceited and jealous, and I haven't taken the time or the trouble to unravel any yarn or run a loom myself for years, and what surprises me is that I should bother to say anything to you at all except go to the devil! Except one thing, that I intended to send that jacket and skirt to you this morning by parcel post!"

Guy Carew was still frowning at her. "The trouble is," he muttered, "the chief trouble is, the kind of man I am. But I'm that kind. I don't know why, either; it isn't a Cherokee trait; the average Cherokee will tell you anything. Maybe it's the mixture. It isn't acquired, for I've always been that way. I was like that when I was a boy, and later at college, and the three years I spent in Europe, and since then among the tribes. I don't think I'm secretive, exactly, it's just a lack of impulse to communicate my own affairs. And then, there really was a reason for me to hesitate to tell anyone why I wanted you to give me that jacket and skirt. Especially —I had no right to burden you with such a confidence."

Jean said drily, "You thought knocking me on the head was better."

"I did not. You know very well I did not. And in any case, I admit I had no right to ask you for it without saying why I wanted it. Another thing, I should have told you why I was sticking close to Portia Tritt."

"Not at all. That's none of *my* business."

"But you seemed to think it was. I mean, the remark you made. When I saw you were jealous—"

"Me? Jealous? My dear fellow—"

"But what you said—"

"What I said? Oh!" Jean laughed. "Now I remember. Maybe I was a little jealous, at the thought of her wearing that costume I had designed for myself."

"Of course. That's what I meant." Guy looked slightly bewildered. "Anyhow, I have an impulse now to communicate my affairs. To you. I want to tell you why I asked you to give me the skirt and jacket, and why I was with Portia Tritt—"

"It isn't at all necessary."

"It is to me. I want to find out who murdered my father. I've told you that much before, but I haven't talked about it. I'm not talking about it now, except to you. It looks as if the police either can't do it or won't, and if they won't I will. Another thing. Look at me, Miss Farris. Please. Have you heard the—the talk that I killed my father myself?"

"Why—" Jean faltered. "I . . . of course some people . . ."

"I know. Lots of people." Blood was at the surface of the smooth tight skin over his cheekbones. "I'm surprised I can talk about it, even with you. They say my father was killed with a war club and scalped, and I'm half Indian. They say he had been giving me half a million a year for my work among the tribes and had decided to stop it. They say he was going to marry Portia Tritt and cut me out of his will. They say one reason I didn't want him to marry Portia Tritt was that I loved her myself. They say I got home from the West on Tuesday, July 6th, and he was killed the next

46

morning." The blood had mounted higher. "You've heard all that?"

Jean nodded and murmured, "Some of it."

"Of course you have." Guy leaned forward at her. "I wouldn't have asked you this before, because it wouldn't have seemed possible . . . but now you say it's possible that I hit you on the head. . . . Do you believe that I killed my father?"

"No."

"Do you think I know who did it or had anything to do with it?"

"No. But . . . that's two questions. You might know who did it."

"I don't. Do you believe me?"

"Yes."

"Good. Now I have to ask you this: Can you conceive of any circumstances in which you would want to marry me?"

Jean's mouth fell open, and immediately closed again. She laughed at little. "Certainly. If we fell in love with each other, and we both had sound bodies and sound minds, and neither of us was otherwise entangled, and we had money enough to pay for a license and a trip to Niagara Falls—"

"I don't mean a joke. You're not in love with me now, are you?"

"Of course not."

"No, of course." He stopped, with his jaw muscles working, and then continued, "The reason I ask is that I'm confused about the code I'm living under. Until I was eight years old I lived among the Cherokees with my father and mother, and with my grandfather, Chief William Straightfoot. My name is Guy Straightfoot Carew. With my schooling in the East and traveling, the culture you were born to has become a part of me, but being born to it is different. I never have any trouble or feeling of strangeness in dealing with men, but I'm never sure with women, nor about them. My mother, Tsianina, died when I was twenty-one, just finishing at Harvard. Maybe you've seen a picture of her?"

Jean nodded. "Lately, in the papers . . . on account of . . ."

"Yes. That has been—" He shrugged. "She was extraordinary. I believe it is correct to suppose that a man's attitude toward women and behavior with them is based on his early intimate experiences with his mother. She sets his tone for life. My mother was a true Indian woman. I don't mean there was any complex or fixation or any of that stuff, but she was my mother and I loved her, and unconsciously she set my tone, and that's what got me confused about the code of my adopted culture. Through reading and so on I know what the rules are, but many of them don't seem natural to me. Still I would like to live up to them. That's what I'm getting at, that I'm trying to observe one of the rules. As I understand it, a man isn't supposed to mention his experiences with women to anyone, except his fiancée under certain circumstances. That's why I want to tell you about Portia Tritt—"

Jean put in hastily, "I'm not your fiancée!"

"I know it. Not yet. But it seems to me that the technical position at any given moment doesn't matter; what's important is the man's intentions. If I can tell my fiancée, why can't I tell a woman I am trying to get for a fiancée, when I need to, to remove difficulties? Isn't that all right?"

"But I—" Jean brushed back her hair. "You've got me confused too. If you mean me . . . of course I know this is just an impersonal discussion . . . I haven't noticed any ardent attempt to get me for a fiancée. One little item, for example, you haven't proposed to me, have you?"

"Certainly not. Didn't you just tell me that you're not in love with me? What good would it do me to propose before you fall in love with me?"

"It might do a lot of good. You're a multimillionaire."

"Rubbish. Would you marry me for money?"

"I would not."

"If I propose to you now, will you accept?"

"I don't like hypothetical questions."

"Will you marry me?"

"No."

"You see." He was frowning at her. "One thing, I don't need to tell you that you can have any amount of fun with me, you see that yourself. I wasn't born for the kind of juggling you can do so well. But that doesn't mean I'm a fool. You know how clever Portia Tritt is. As near as I can judge, she's the cleverest woman I've ever known."

"She's plenty clever enough."

"Yes, she is. But though it was eight years ago, in Paris, when I was only twenty-three, it only took me a week to see that she—but I suppose I'm talking like a cad? It's next to impossible for me to tell. Since you were born to it, I suppose you can't realize how difficult it is to know what is being a cad and what isn't. The nuances are very fine. Is it all right for me to go on?"

"I don't think so." Jean brushed back her hair again. "Not that you're a cad, but it isn't necessary, and even if I were your fiancée I wouldn't require an explanation of anything that happened eight years ago. Just to lessen your confusion, I might add that it would be quite different if it were something happening now."

Guy regarded her. After a moment he said, "I see. You mean you would like me to explain why I was with Portia Tritt yesterday. That's what—"

"I don't mean that at all! You certainly could do with a little more understanding of women, Mr. Carew!"

"I know I could. Anyway, that's what I was going to do next, and I'm sure this isn't being a cad. I was with her yesterday, and I've been a great deal with her the past four weeks, because I want to learn who murdered my father."

Jean stared. "You don't think she knows!"

"I think she knows something, I don't know what. She was there, in the house. She was going to marry my father. And on the morning he was killed, immediately after he was killed, she did something very peculiar, and her explanation for it isn't satisfactory. And . . I did something peculiar that morning myself. I said I'm not a fool, but I begin to believe that what I did that morning was foolish. I . . . I'd rather not tell you. I'm sure it was foolish. So that's why I was with Portia Tritt yesterday."

"She didn't look—" Jean bit her lip.

"She didn't look what?"

"Nothing."

He gazed at her, and shrugged. "All right. Then about asking you to give me the skirt and jacket—"

"You don't need to explain—"

"Pardon me, I do need to. Something happened yesterday morning and Wednesday afternoon. A newspaper reporter called on everyone who was at Lucky Hills that night—Buysse, Wilson, Kranz, Barth and his wife, Portia Tritt. He couldn't find me Wednesday and so I was the last. He asked for information regarding a garment that had bayeta yarn in it—a jacket, sweater, anything; and he said that the police had found, clutched in my father's left hand, a piece of bayeta yarn which he had evidently pulled from the clothing of his murderer. They had kept that clue secret. He wanted to know if any of us owned such a garment or knew of anyone who did."

Jean, her eyes fastened on his face, murmured, "Bayeta?"

"So he said. I phoned my lawyer, Orlik, at once, and he went to see the district attorney. The district attorney was sore but that wouldn't faze Orlik, and he got it that the reporter was right. The yarn had been clutched in my father's left hand, and the police had learned that it was genuine bayeta.

In that case, my father's murderer was wearing my jacket. The one I later gave to you."

"But—" Jean's eyes were wide and fixed. She put out a hand and then let it drop to the table. "But you don't know that. One little piece of yarn—and you haven't seen it—"

Guy said grimly, "I don't need to. The police wouldn't make a mistake on a thing like that, and if it was bayeta it was from my jacket. Bayeta blankets are too rare and costly to make clothes from. I told you about my jacket. It was made for me last spring by a Choctaw woman from a piece of blanket she had, because I got her son out of jail. I brought it east with me. I had it outdoors that afternoon, the afternoon of July 6th, at the tennis court, but I thought I took it back to the house and put it in the closet in the side hall where the balls and rackets are kept. Not that I looked for it, for the next morning my father was found murdered. It may have been there all the time, but I suppose it wasn't or the police would have found it; they must have been secretly searching for something with bayeta in it. Anyhow, the next time I saw it was the afternoon two weeks ago that I drove you to Lucky Hills. You remember when I was showing you the house and took you to my room to look at some Indian stuff, the jacket was there in a chair and I was surprised to see it? And we discussed it and I gave it to you, and you took it with you that evening?"

Jean nodded. "I remember."

"All right, the murderer wore that jacket. I don't know where it had been those two weeks. I don't know who put it on the chair in my room."

"Someone's trying—someone wants you accused—"

"Maybe. But why was it put in my room, where I would almost certainly be the first to see it? And if it was known to be mine, why wait two weeks to produce it?"

"Who knew it was yours?"

"Buysse and Wilson. I had shown it to them, with other things I had brought. They are my friends, and of course wouldn't tell the newspaper reporter. I don't think Barth or his wife could have known, if they saw it on me that afternoon, or they would have told the reporter—unless—" He stopped. In a moment he went on, "But I think not. If that was it Barth would be after me. I don't know about Kranz and Portia Tritt; they had seen it, and they know textiles. I don't know. Anyhow, you see why I said I wanted to explain. I had to, and besides, I have to ask a favor of you. Three of them. The first is, have you any of that bayeta left, any at all?"

"A very little. Scraps."

"Would you give me a piece of it?"

Jean proceeded to prove that Miss Delaney had been right in deciding that the chaos was not disorder. She went straight to a large filing cabinet against the wall, opened the third section from the top, fingered in it a few seconds, and withdrew a manila folder. She recrossed and handed the folder to Guy.

"Take it all if you want it."

"No, thanks, I just want a piece." He pulled out a thread of yarn some ten inches long, inspected it and tucked it into his pocket, and handed the folder back to Jean. As she was returning it to the cabinet she observed over her shoulder:

"You said three favors."

"Yes. The second is this." He hesitated, waited until she had returned to her stool, and then resumed, "I don't like to ask it. It's the sort of thing—for instance, if you were my fiancée I wouldn't mind."

"Well, it's too bad, but I'm not. Go ahead."

"I suppose I'll have to. I must. It is extremely important—that is, important to me—that no one be told a word of this—the jacket, the yarn—"

"I'm not quite a fool either," Jean said shortly. "No one will be told by me."

"I know it's asking a good deal—"

"Not at all. What's the third favor?"

"The police may even come and question you—it's entirely my fault that that may happen and I owe you—"

"Nonsense. Let them question. Though I don't see why they should come to me if no one is to be told."

"That's what I'm coming to. They may come to you and they may not. But there were twenty people at that dinner table last evening. Mrs. Barth told us, after we had signed what we had written and she had collected the papers, that she was going to give the papers to you. Did she? And may I see them?"

For a tenth of a second Jean looked blank. Then she exclaimed, "Oh! Of course! Yes, I have them. But I don't see—how can they be—"

She stopped, and gaped at him. She jumped from the stool and took two steps towards him.

"Good God! Guy! Whoever knocked me on the head and stole my clothes—that was the murderer!"

Involuntarily she put up her palm and pressed it against her head, above the ear, and stood, still staring.

VI

As regards accessibility, the man in that room might have been the Minotaur in its lair. To reach him, it was necessary first to say to the elevator man: "Forty, please," or, "Barth & Pomeroy"; then to accost the young woman at the reception desk; then to confer with the young man who would appear from within; then, if you got that far, to withstand the searching eyes of the sharp-nosed woman to whose presence you had penetrated; and then to wait. It could be done, with exceptional credentials and sufficient patience and a careful avoidance of sudden or suspicious movements.

The room itself was spacious, luxuriously carpeted, furnished with desk and chairs and accessories of Brazilian Mura, and windowed to the west and south. Friday morning at eleven, the man behind the desk was the one who belonged there, Melville Barth; the bulky one seated across from him, with a cigar in his teeth, was Inspector Cramer of the homicide squad.

Cramer was saying, "I understand that, and I'm much obliged. I got on the case only yesterday, and I wanted it firsthand. A rumor's only a rumor, no matter whether it's Flatbush backyard or Wall Street. You say that you and Carew reached an agreement that Tuesday night."

"I do." Barth was obviously under restraint. "He wasn't as hard as I had feared he would be. It was no rumor and no secret that I was caught on Western Chemical, the whole Street knew it. Carew had the only door out for me, and he was as decent as I had any right to expect. Now I'm still in, with Guy Carew and the damned lawyers to deal with. I suppose I can't blame the boy for hesitating to ignore their advice; he doesn't know the ropes. But as far as my interests are concerned, I wish to God whoever killed Carew had waited another twenty-four hours."

"Your agreement with him wasn't in writing?"

"You don't write that sort of thing."

"No memorandum at all?"

"No."

Cramer removed his cigar and sat. Finally he grumbled, "All right. You're a man of affairs, you know what inconvenience a murder means to anyone with enough bad luck to be within range. It was a little after midnight when you and Carew got through?"

"Around a quarter after."

"And you went right upstairs and to bed?"

"I did. My wife and I occupied the same room. I slept well; I always do. I wanted to get away fairly early, and at 7:30 I was up and taking a shower. I was dressed and ready to go down to breakfast, waiting for my wife, when Guy Carew came to our door with the news and said the police would soon be there. I heard nothing and saw nothing that could possibly have been connected with the murder."

"Tell me exactly what young Carew said when he came to your door."

This installment of the inconvenience to Mr. Barth had begun at ten o'clock, and it was not over until noon, for Inspector Cramer was tickling the frog without the faintest notion of which way it would jump. With Barth he was exhibiting patience and consideration, but also persistence and thoroughness. He chewed up three cigars, went over the same ground time and again, and paid no attention when Barth got restive and sharp. But finally he dropped the third cigar in the tray, got up and grunted barely adequate appreciation, and departed.

Barth sat some minutes and then reached to push a button. Almost at once a door opened and the sharp-nosed woman appeared. Her searching eyes still searched, even when directed at her employer.

"Well?" she inquired.

Barth shook his head. "I didn't tell him. I know, Rachel, I can't remember once in twenty years that your advice hasn't been good . . . but I didn't tell him. Not that I see how I can possibly use it. I can't very well go to Guy Carew and say that when my wife and I arrived at Lucky Hills that afternoon we saw him coming from the tennis court wearing a jacket with red yarn in it, and that I may or may not report that fact to the police. Can I? Damn it. Sit down."

At 2:00 P.M. Inspector Cramer stood just inside the door of the tomb of Tsianina on the Lucky Hills estate of Valentine Carew—now of his son Guy Carew—and with a slow revolving glance surveyed the imposing ensemble. He had been moving fast. His lunch had been three cheese sandwiches and a bottle of beer, consumed on the back seat of his official limousine as it speeded north with the speedometer steady at sixty. He had gone over the Lucky Hills house, with special attention to the location of the rooms which the guests and inmates had occupied on the night of July 6th, and to exits and entrances, and had briefly questioned a dozen servants.

He turned to the man on his right, a Westchester assistant district attorney who had come from White Plains to bring the key to the tomb. "Everything is back in place?"

The man nodded. "With the greatest care. You know how the law protects the home of the dead. Except the knife and the war club. We have those."

Cramer nodded, and turned to the man on his left. It was the old Indian, Woodrow Wilson. He was wearing a blue cotton shirt with a red bow tie, blue overalls with a bib, and white canvas shoes, all immaculate. Cramer said, "Show me how the body was when you found it."

The Indian stepped to a spot some eight paces from the door, and pointed straight down to the floor. "Head." His finger moved to an angle. "Feet."

"Did you touch him?"

"I touch him a little. I lift one eye open."

"Was it closed?"

"Not closed, no." The Indian shrugged. "Not open either."

"Did you move him?"

"No."

"Those masonry steps and the platform—were they where they are now?"

"No. Back maybe ten feet."

The Inspector looked around again. Skinner had been correct; it was impressive. They had left the door standing open; otherwise the light would have been even dimmer than it was. The room was enormous, and nearly as high as it was wide. The holes in the east wall, through which the morning sun could come, or not come, for Tsianina's dead answer to her husband's living question, were now, looking up from the floor, shadowy outlines of circles. Everywhere else the walls were covered with thousands of objects, large and small, imperfectly seen, and at both sides were rows of large glass cabinets.

The Indian said unexpectedly, with a tone of pride, "Everything in here is Cherokee."

Cramer mounted the stone steps, counting from habit. There were twenty-eight of them—the days of the moon, though he did not know it. From the top of the massive platform, he found that he could look directly through one of the holes to daylight if he stooped; and, by moving his head, another and another; then he stopped as his head touched the edge of the casket which rested on a stone slab. He raised his head a little and peered through the glass lid, and saw Tsianina. From her chin down she was covered with what he knew to be a garment of willow-tanned doeskin, since it was a public fact; he could barely see that it was there; but there was dim light on her face, and he saw with a sort of astonishment that he would have recognized it from her pictures. It was not waxen or deathlike, in that soft gloom; it was not even unnatural; it was merely remote and beautiful.

The voice of the assistant district attorney sounded: "We had to string some lights. Shall I turn them on?"

"No!" Cramer exploded hastily, and descended the steps. Near the door again he said, "I had to see it, of course, but there's no use wasting time, since your men have gone over it with microscopes. Where's the lance with the prints?"

"It's at White Plains too. It hung there." He pointed. "And on that cabinet yonder. Do you think there's anything to that?"

"I haven't even begun to think." The inspector was at the great brass door. Grasping its handle, he swung it on its hinges until it was closed, and then opened it in again. Twice more he swung it back and forth; it moved in perfect silence. He grunted. "I guess Carew wouldn't have heard it opening, at that. Let's go outside."

They passed out and the White Plains man turned the key in the lock and put it in his pocket. Cramer said something to the Indian and was led across the closely clipped turf to a gap in the high yew hedge which was the beginning of an alley leading without the enclosure. The Indian pointed. "There."

"Show me how you were standing."

The Indian moved to a position about a foot to the left of the gap, and stood.

"You were hit on top of the head?"

"No. Here." The Indian tapped with a finger on the left of his skull, back of the ear.

"Carew was inside the tomb and the door was open?"

"No. Closed."

"Was the sun shining?"

"Yes. Bright sun."

"While you stood here, with Carew inside the tomb, what were you thinking about?"

"Me?" A grunt, possibly derisive. "Not thinking."

"Were you thinking that Carew had forgot the Princess Tsianina and was going to marry another woman?"

The Indian shrugged and shook his head. The assistant

district attorney yawned without restraint, and Cramer turned to him with mild sarcasm: "You bored?"

"No—but this damn Indian. We had him for two weeks. Your men have tried him too. You say you've read the reports?"

"Yeah, I know." Cramer gazed at the face of Woodrow Wilson—the dark furrowed skin that had never felt a razor, the knobs of the cheekbones, the slits of the eyes. Abruptly he blurted at him, "Yesterday afternoon you went to see Barth. What for?"

The Indian nodded without hesitation and said, "Yesterday. To eat."

"I said yesterday. What did you want to see Barth about?"

"Not to see Mr. Barth. My friend Mr. Buysse took me for a ride and we went there. Among so many people you would not see me hardly. A thousand people there—more than that, two hundred. Some stayed to eat and I stayed with my friend. Mrs. Barth said by all means stay. Maybe you know Cherokee life and thoughts about woman? Always the house is the woman's house. Whatever she say in the house you do it. If she say stay and eat and you go, bad insult. If woman gets insult in the house—"

"I see. That's fine. Did you go there to see Mrs. Barth?"

"Me?" The slits of Wilson's eyes widened a fraction of an inch. "Hell, no. More fact about Cherokee life: A man never go see woman of another man in her house, never if man there. If a man want to see that woman his eyes tell her where, or maybe he wait till the dance and then tell her. She say yes come or she say not come, but never her house. For that reason me not go see Mrs. Barth. But she say stay and eat—"

"Yeah, you said that. You listen to me. You understand a plain question, don't you? You're damn right you do. You went to Barth's house to see someone. *Who?*"

Wilson shrugged. "Too many people there. See Mr. Kranz, woman Portia Tritt. See Guy Straightfoot Carew, son of Tsianina. See my friend Mr. Buysse, reason I ride with him. See woman with yellow eyes, bright red dress, little feet. Mr. Buysse said come on and ride, what the hell, nice day to ride. Then not what I expect, Mrs. Barth said stay and eat. More fact about Cherokee life—"

Cramer demanded of the White Plains man, "Did you fellows work on this specimen for two weeks?"

"Off and on. Nothing had any effect. If you stuck him in boiling oil up to his waist it would remind him of more fact about Cherokee life."

Cramer grunted in disgust. "I'll see him again later. Now I'm just meeting folks and getting the picture. At present I'm willing to get a bet down on Commissioner Humbert's choice."

"Me?"

Two heads jerked around at the Indian who, judging from his tone, intended it for a polite question. Cramer stared at him a second, growled, "For God's sake," and strode off.

The inspector was still moving fast. At four o'clock he had telephoned twice to his office and given detailed instructions regarding a new development that had presented itself, phoned also to the commissioner and the district attorney, been driven south again as far as the National Indian Museum on Ninety-third Street and spent half an hour with its director, Amory Buysse, and was still there.

They sat together in the director's modest but attractive office at the rear of the museum's third floor, which contained implements and clothing of the Mackenzie and California areas. Cramer had actually got something: a peach seed, now reposing in his pocket, and a recital of its history. The mystery of Woodrow Wilson being taken for a ride to the house of Mrs. Barth had been cleared up; and Buysse had further stated that he had been aware that his car had been followed on that occasion but that he had been undisturbed by the fact, because he had got used to it. Buysse had also recapitulated briefly but patiently his answers to thousands of previous questions. His invitation for dinner and to spend the night of July 6th at Lucky Hills was nothing out of the ordinary; all the conferences regarding the affairs of the museum had taken place in that manner; besides, he was Val Carew's oldest friend and Carew had continued to enjoy his company. He had arrived at Lucky Hills at six o'clock, chatted for an hour with Guy Carew, who had just returned from the West, dined with the others, smoked a couple of cigars on one of the terraces with Guy and Woodrow Wilson, and gone up to bed a little before midnight, to the room he always occupied when there. He had slept well, had heard or seen nothing unusual, and had not again left his room before 7:40, when Wilson had come to his door to tell him that Carew had been found murdered. Yes, while smoking on the terrace they had discussed the probability that Carew would marry Portia Tritt, but none of them had expressed undue resentment. The subject had been opened by questions from Guy, who had in fact come East in some haste because it had been suggested in a letter which had been written him by Buysse. They had agreed that such a marriage would be unfortunate, but certainly there had been no thought of active interference to prevent it. Their chief concern, in fact, had been for the weather. July 7th was the birthday of Tsianina; it had been the custom of Val Carew to reserve important questions for her answer on that morning, by the rays of the sun on her face or their absence; which would it be? He was sure, Buysse said, that the only action any of that trio had in mind was the action of the heavens; they wanted sunshine and plenty of it. Yes, Val Carew would actually have permitted such a question to find its answer in that manner.

What did Buysse know of an affair, eight years ago in Paris, between Guy Carew and Portia Tritt?

Nothing whatever, and he didn't want to.

What did he know of the friendship between Portia Tritt and Leo Kranz?

Nothing whatever, and he wasn't interested.

Or of the conversation that night, ending after midnight, between Val Carew and Melville Barth?

Nothing whatever.

Was it true that Carew had told him, Buysse, that in case he married again his annual contribution to the National Indian Museum would be stopped or greatly decreased?

No, and neither was it true that a skunk doesn't smell.

But hadn't Buysse perhaps suspected such a result from Carew's marriage to a young and handsome woman?

No.

But hadn't Buysse admitted that he regarded such a marriage as unfortunate?

Buysse said, "Listen, mister. You aiming to get me mad? What for?"

Cramer passed it by. He chewed his cigar a while and then suddenly demanded, "When Wilson came to your room to report the murder, what did he say?"

"You mean the exact words?"

"If you remember, yes."

"Well—something like this: 'The young one say come to tomb. Tsianina's man dead.'"

"'The young one' meaning Guy?"

"That's right."

"Did Wilson look grief-stricken?"

"No. If you've seen him you know how he looks. He never looks different."

"Why didn't he go back to the tomb with you?"

"Because he was groggy. He had been knocked cold, and

he's an old man. I made him lie down on my bed and then beat it."

"When you got to the tomb, what was Kranz doing?"

"Standing there."

"What did you and he do while you were waiting?"

"I took a look at Val Carew and then I sat down on the stone steps and stayed there. Kranz stood over by the door."

"No talking?"

"I didn't feel like talking. I don't know whether Kranz did or not."

"How long did you wait?"

"I guess I had been there about ten minutes when Guy came. It was fifteen minutes more before the police arrived. More came soon after. There was nothing I could do, and I started to leave, when one of the cops—I believe his name was Captain Goss—asked Guy and Kranz and me if we would object to being searched. I couldn't see any sense in that, under the circumstances, but none of us objected. They went over us one by one, and made a list of what we had on us, and then I went to the house to see how Wilson was. Before I left, Barth and Miss Tritt had arrived."

"I've seen that list. I noticed you had a piece of carved bone in your pocket and you said it was a Dakota battle charm. Do you always carry that?"

"No. Guy had brought back some stuff from the West and had given me that for the museum. It's downstairs now if you want to take a look at it."

"Much obliged." Cramer sat moodily eying the museum director with his lips screwed up, and after a moment abruptly switched: "Did you ever see a man scalped?"

Buysse shook his head. "Nope, I never did."

"Then you don't know how hard it would be to pull it off."

"Are you asking me how hard it would be?"

"Say I am."

Buysse grunted. "Then you're a hell of a detective. How would I know? As it happens, I do know. I asked a doctor. He said it would come off easy if you used a sharp knife, but if you only used the knife to carve the circle and then pulled it would take quite some jerk." Buysse leaned back. "My friend Peterson at the American Museum says you folks have been asking him about scalping habits—which tribes took it all and which ones took only a part and so on. That's all goose feathers. I mean that scalping stunt. Forget it. I can see how it would strike you. Wilson's an Indian, and Guy Carew is part Indian, and so when they killed a man they would scalp him. Well, maybe they might. But so might anyone else if they wanted to make it look like an Indian."

"Yeah, I thought of that alone."

"I suppose you did. Another thing, that business about a piece of bayeta yarn in Val's hand. A newspaperman was here a couple of days ago, and one of your men yesterday. People don't wear things made of bayeta. But anyone who knows about it could have got a strand of it from a blanket and closed Val's fingers over it after they killed him. There are three bayeta blankets at Lucky Hills. There are eight in this museum."

"Uh-huh, I thought of that too, but I don't like it much."

"You don't? Why not?"

"Oh, I just don't. But this scalping stunt, I'd like to ask a few more questions about that. . . ."

District Attorney Skinner sat in his office sidewise to his desk, with his eyes narrowed at the man who was in a chair facing him. The visitor, medium-sized and gray-haired, was tailored and outfitted with expensive care and the best of taste, and would have been notable anywhere for his shrewd steadfast eyes, as pale as ice.

Skinner broke a silence, suavely, choosing his words. "No, Orlik, I don't say it's unethical. I only say I'm surprised that a man of your standing would suggest such a thing. You know very well the police can't permit valuable evidence, especially in a murder case, to be examined by anyone who takes a fancy—"

"Not fancy." The visitor gestured impatiently. "I'm aware that I'm not representing a defendant, with a legal right to enforce, because there is no defendant, since you've made no charge. But they took that Indian on a fishing expedition up in Westchester, and kept him two weeks, didn't they? And all the time they had that piece of yarn and kept it quiet. Wilson is still my client, and he is still in jeopardy, and you know it. How do I know when you'll nab him again? So is Buysse my client, and Mr. Guy Carew, and they are all being kept under surveillance. Must they submit indefinitely to that annoyance? Now that your finding that piece of yarn in the dead man's hand has been made public—"

"We didn't publish it."

"All the worse. You should either have published it or defended it. Instead, it was permitted to trickle out in a manner most damaging to the repute of respectable citizens. Now you insinuate that it would be contrary to the ends of justice to allow me to have the yarn examined by an accredited expert in my employ."

"Not at all." Skinner remained suave. "I merely say it isn't necessary. It has been examined by three of the best experts available. They agree that it is genuine bayeta."

"That means very little."

"Why?"

"Because bayeta is a very broad term. The whole period during which those blankets were being woven extends to nearly two centuries. Between any two specimens now extant, the yarn always shows a variation, sometimes minute, sometimes apparent even to a novice. So to say that the yarn is bayeta doesn't mean much. But say—just as a hypothesis —say that I have in my possession a strand of bayeta taken from one of the blankets at Lucky Hills or in the National Indian Museum, and an expert is permitted to compare it microscopically with your specimen. He can tell with a high degree of certainty whether they came from the same source."

"No doubt." Skinner's eyes narrowed. Then he smiled. "I see no reason, Orlik, why you shouldn't be told—just between us. What you suggest has been done. Our piece of bayeta has been compared with over fifty specimens collected from various places—including the two you mentioned. Oh, we were careful about it, and circumspect—we didn't injure valuable property. The experts tell us we haven't found *the* source. But your taking the trouble to come—as busy a man as you—makes me wonder—do you have a strand of bayeta in your possession?"

"I said a hypothesis."

"I know, but do you?"

"I could easily have several."

"Of course you could, but do you have one? One in particular with which you would like to compare ours?"

The lawyer smiled. "If I have, and if you let me compare them, you could ask that question again."

"I'd rather ask it now." Skinner's voice was oiled. "It's a murder case, Orlik. A mean thing to monkey with, no matter what your professional standing may be. And you're not very discerning to play me for a fool. Did you really think I'd be ass enough to let you get your hands on that piece of evidence?"

"Not my hands. An accredited expert. On your premises. In the presence of your men."

"Then you admit that you have in your possession a piece of bayeta which you suspect—"

"I admit nothing. I came here to ask a professional courtesy. I would appreciate it. Mr. Guy Carew would apprec—"

"Appreciate hell!" The district attorney leaned forward and slapped his palm on the desk. "Listen, Orlik! By God, if you have got some yarn that came from the same place our piece came from—and you have the nerve to come here and start bellyaching about the ends of justice—"

Mr. Orlik was standing up. He faintly smiled, and held out his hand. Skinner, with a jerk, swiveled away from him. Orlik smiled again, and went.

VII

Leo Kranz, having locked the door, led the way to the rear of the gallery, where there were comfortable chairs and a smoking stand, and gestured his caller to a seat. "Now," he said, "we won't be disturbed. I'm sorry, but that was an important customer. It isn't often, in August, that someone walks in and selects three thousand dollars' worth of old French prints. And two of my assistants are on vacation and the third is ill. . . ."

Inspector Cramer mumbled something and shook his head at a proffered cigarette box of ivory, and glanced again at his wrist watch. "I'm a little pressed for time," he declared. "Suppose you tell me briefly in your own words. I understand you were a frequent guest at Lucky Hills?"

Kranz nodded. "I first met Carew about fifteen years ago. I used to have a little place up north of Mount Kisco, not far from his estate, and we got into the habit of playing billiards together and we hit it off pretty well. I liked him, and I think I can say he liked me. Of recent years I've been there often, in the summer."

"Was there anything special about your visit on July 6th?"

"Special?"

"Well—it was Tuesday. Not a weekend."

"Oh. No, nothing special. I went sometimes in the middle of the week."

"Nothing, for instance, in connection with Carew's intention to marry Portia Tritt?"

"No." Kranz flicked ash from his cigarette. "Why?"

Cramer shrugged. "We just ask questions, because we

have to. You know how that is, Mr. Kranz. I understand you got there around five o'clock."

"About that. I left early and motored up. I played a little tennis with Guy, then Buysse and the Barths came—Miss Tritt was already there—and there were some cocktails. After dinner Miss Tritt and I played billiards. Carew was off somewhere with Barth, and I think the others were out on the terrace. I told Miss Tritt good night a little after eleven and went up to bed. I was up and dressed early—I'm an early riser and I always want coffee as soon as I'm up—and at half past seven I was sitting on the east terrace drinking coffee when Wilson, the old Indian, passed by, and I thought he looked odd. I followed him in the house, thinking I don't know what, because I had never seen such a look on his face and I had known him a long time. He went upstairs. In a little while he came down and Guy was with him. Guy said his father had been killed and told me to come along, and told Wilson to go back in and tell Buysse. We ran, and by the time we reached the tomb Guy was thirty yards ahead of me. Carew was there—"

Kranz stopped. Cramer waited. In a moment Kranz went on. "I'm emotional. I suppose I'm hyper something. When I speak of it I see it again—and feel it again—I can't help it. Carew was there dead. We saw at once he was dead. Guy asked me to stay there and he went back to the house. In about ten minutes Buysse arrived, and we remained there together. The police came—a couple of the state police—at five minutes after eight."

Cramer sighed, and began questions. He knew that Kranz had answered them all before, and he knew what the answers had been, but he had to get acquainted with these people as the first step in his effort to send one of them—or two or three—to the electric chair. So he asked questions, and found that although Kranz might be emotional, he was also a man of sense. He agreed with the inspector that if he himself had had a desire to murder Carew, he could easily have got to the tomb unobserved at that early hour, knocked the Indian out, entered the tomb and performed the deed, and returned to the house to sit on the terrace and ask the butler for coffee. He also agreed that any of the guests might have done the same thing, leaving the house by the door at the end of the corridor of the north wing, unlocking the door from the inside and locking it again upon returning.

More questions. Kranz was as patient as Barth and Buysse had been, even when Cramer abruptly inquired:

"When did you first learn that there was a bequest to you of a couple of hundred thousand in Carew's will?"

"When the will was made public."

"Carew had never told you?"

"No. If I had thought about it I might have expected it, for he was a generous man, but he never mentioned it." Kranz frowned. "I know there's no point in getting indignant about implications, but it does seem that by this time you might have eliminated the possibility that I killed him for the money I would get. Even if I had known of it. My affairs are in excellent condition. I have no need of money. Haven't you found that out?"

Cramer admitted that they had, and added that he had intended no implication. "It is merely," he explained, "the necessary technic of investigation. I haven't the slightest reason to suspect that you murdered your friend Val Carew to get the money he had left you in his will. I don't even think it's credible. But I ask you anyway whether you knew about it before he died. You say 'No.' What if later, when I'm talking with Portia Tritt for instance, I am told that you discussed with her, previous to Carew's death, the legacy you expected from him and mentioned the amount? You see. There's no use resenting implications when there aren't any. And by the way, speaking of Miss Tritt, what was your attitude toward her contemplated marriage?"

"Well." Kranz crushed a cigarette in the tray. "I didn't like it."

"Why not?"

"Various reasons. For one thing, he was twice her age. Val was over sixty."

"Did you discuss it with him?"

"Not much. Once or twice."

"Have an argument?"

"No, I wouldn't call it an argument. You didn't argue with him regarding his personal projects. He made his own decisions—that is, he had his own way of making them."

"Was he really nut enough to leave an important decision to that contraption in the tomb? Sunshine through a hole in the wall?"

"He wasn't a nut. To an unbeliever, a saint's relic is garbage. To a Christian, Mecca is an unsanitary town full of fleas. A man who has a shrine has transcended reason."

"Uh-huh. But about the marriage. What other reasons did you have for not liking it?"

Kranz waved a hand. "I gave you the most important one. For another—I had a selfish one. Miss Tritt is one of the most accomplished stylists and publicity counselors in New York. I am one of her accounts. She has handled publicity for my textile business for four years, and for this gallery for over a year, and she is extremely good. I didn't want to lose her."

"Any others?"

"No." Kranz smiled a little. "That was enough. I've admitted my selfishness. Of course you've discovered that I wasn't alone in disapproving of that proposed marriage—but that's an old story. I don't suppose it has ever happened that a man over sixty marrying an attractive young woman has met with approval from anyone, except the couple themselves. But it isn't often that the disapproval is sufficiently strong to cause a resort to murder."

"Does that mean that you think there was another motive for the murder?"

"Not at all. I am as much at sea as—well, as you are, apparently."

Cramer grunted. "I'm not even floating yet, I'm just shoving off. That's why I have to ask you a lot of questions you have already answered. For instance, did Carew ever mention to you an intention to stop his support of the National Indian Museum?"

"No."

"Or to curtail it?"

"No."

"Did you ever hear such an intention discussed by Carew or Buysse or anyone else?"

"No."

The inspector went on asking questions which had already been answered.

At five o'clock, which was about the time Leo Kranz was locking the door of his gallery for a tête-à-tête with Inspector Cramer, Eileen Delaney was sitting at her desk in her own little office at the premises of Jean Farris Fabrics. It was not at all chaotic, but was fairly filled with filing cabinets, stacks of magazines and papers, miscellany, and a couple of chairs. She looked up from a sheet of figures she was studying as the door opened and the chunky little woman from the anteroom appeared.

"A man named Parker from a newspaper."

"What newspaper?"

"He wouldn't say. He says he spoke to Miss Farris at the street door as she was going out."

"Send him in."

Cora went. In a few moments the door opened again, and a man entered. The fact that Miss Delaney had again bent over the sheet of figures with a frown of concentration gave him an opportunity to appraise her with a keener glance than, presumably, he would otherwise have permitted himself. He was medium-sized and carelessly dressed, with a wide mouth and full lips, a small nose, and lively dark eyes which seemed to change expression instantaneously as Miss Delaney looked up.

She demanded, brusquely but amicably, "You're somebody new? I never saw you before, did I?"

He shook his head apologetically. "I'm not in the trade line, Miss Delaney. As a matter of fact, I'm not on a newspaper at all. I'm a free lance, and I want to propose a piece of publicity—"

"Our publicity is handled by—"

"Sure, I know. Ethel Gannon. As I said, I'm not in the trade line, but I know the ropes and I get around. I know you're highly specialized and none of the ordinary junk would interest you, but what I have to propose is a natural for the *Town and Country Register* and I have a connection there. I wanted to discuss it with Miss Farris, but she was leaving just as I came in, and she said for me to see you." He had got to the desk and opened his portfolio on it, and now swiftly extracted something and handed it across. "What do you think of that?"

Miss Delaney took it and saw a glossy—a snapshot of a group of people on a lawn under trees. It was a good shot, but having seen thousands of others as good, she demanded merely, "Well?"

"Well," the man smiled, "of course I know you couldn't do anything very special just with that. It's a good picture of Miss Jean Farris in a new fall ensemble on the lawn of Mr. and Mrs. Melville Barth's country home, and the rotos would use it, but that's not what I'm after. What I want, and what I can get with your cooperation, is a page spread in the *Tee and See*. As you know, it was taken yesterday."

"Where did you get it?"

"From one of the boys. As I said, I know the ropes. That outfit Miss Farris was wearing created a sensation yesterday afternoon—but of course she told you about it?"

"I don't know that she did. It's been a busy day here."

The lids of the man's eyes had drooped a little—against the light? They opened again. "Well, it did. I want to do a piece—for one thing, one thing that would help—could I see it? On a model would do—or even just see it—if it happens to be handy—"

Miss Delaney shook her head. "It isn't here. I suppose it's at Miss Farris's apartment, since she wore it home."

"I wanted to see it." The man looked disappointed. He picked up the glossy, glanced at it, and tossed it to the desk again. "It's a good picture, anyway. And what I really want is something else, to make a story out of it. That's what I'm good at, I see a story that other people miss. Yesterday afternoon everybody was interested when Miss Farris told about the bayeta yarn in that ensemble, but do you think any of the press girls had the sense to pick it up? Not a one. They all muffed it. It was a good-looking outfit and all that, but the real story is in that bayeta yarn. Think of it! The dye made in Persia, and the yarn in Spain, three centuries ago! The Indians killing the Spanish soldiers, and taking their uniforms and unraveling them, and weaving the yarn into blankets! And now, in the twentieth century, the foremost designer in America using that same yarn in a fashionable ensemble that makes a sensation at an exclusive garden party showing! Tell me that's not a story? It's a natural for the *Tee and See!*"

Miss Delaney smiled a little. She was fully aware of the sweet uses of publicity, especially when the proposed medium was of the nature of the *Town and Country Register*. She looked with calculating interest at the lively dark eyes and inquired, "And you want something from this end too? I'm afraid you'll have to see Miss Gannon—"

"Not at all." The man sounded a little hurt. "I'm no hog. I'll get mine from the *Tee and See*. But I need your cooperation to make it as good as I can. This picture of the ensemble is plenty good enough, and it's a good shot of Miss Farris too, but what I want is a piece of the bayeta yarn itself, shoot it, enlarge it maybe six times, and print it the length of the page. That's why I was hoping the outfit was here, I thought maybe we could take a strand of the yarn from it. Of course I could fake it, but that would be dangerous, especially in an enlargement. I doubt if I would dare do it if I didn't have the real thing. What would do just as well —if you have a piece of it left over—do you?"

"I'm not sure." Miss Delaney pursed her lips. "Miss Farris always keeps a sample, but I don't know whether she had any of that left or not. She'll be here in the morning—"

"I wouldn't like to wait. This is hot. Maybe you could look —if it isn't too much trouble. . . ."

Miss Delaney hesitated. She never liked to discuss publicity with her partner anyway, for although Jean had sense enough to understand its necessity, she shied off whenever she could. And this was certainly decorous and dignified enough. . . .

She got up, asked the man to wait, and passed through the intervening room into Jean's sanctum. There she again received proof that the chaos was not disorder. First she consulted a large canvas-bound book, speedily found the entry she sought, and went to a filing cabinet and opened the third section from the top. The folder she extracted after a little fingering bore an inscription in Jean's bold hand on an outside flap: "7/21/37—Bayeta—GC—unr by JF—9 oz.—to Krone for JF."

Miss Delaney, frowning at it, muttered to herself, "Is that so, G. C., I didn't know that—if she didn't want me to, she shouldn't have put it here in the open file—anyway, I don't see what difference it makes so long as it's bayeta—"

She selected a single strand the length of three fingers, returned the yarn to the folder, and the folder to the file.

In her office, she was surprised to see the man sitting at her desk, writing with her pen on a piece of her paper. He looked up and smiled apologetically, and hastily arose.

"Did you find it?" He reached for the yarn, eagerly, but not too eagerly. "That's fine! So that's real bayeta! It is a story, you know—it's a peach!" He tucked the yarn into a pocket, and extended a piece of paper. "I took the liberty of using your desk—I hope you won't mind—if you'll just sign that—"

She looked at it. It was a Jean Farris Fabrics letterhead, and he had written the date on it and the sentence: *I hereby certify that this yarn is a piece of the genuine bayeta used in weaving the material for the costume worn by Miss Jean Farris on the afternoon of August 5, 1937.*

She glanced up quickly at the lively dark eyes and caught the lids drooping again. She had a mild protest ready, but he was ahead of her, explaining:

"My reputation is pretty fair, but after all, it would be simple for me to get a piece of red yarn somewhere and call it bayeta, and the *Tee and See* editors aren't experts. Of course, don't sign it if you'd rather not, but it would make it a little easier for me to put it over. . . ."

Miss Delaney shrugged, sat at her desk, and reached for her pen.

Down on the street, five minutes later, a taxi driver got a signal from the sidewalk and swerved to the curb. An agile medium-sized man with a portfolio under his arm hopped in and slammed the door to.

"Police Headquarters, Centre Street."

The driver grunted and shifted gears. The passenger leaned forward: "Step on it. Fifteen minutes ought to do it. Make it hot, and don't worry. Here." The passenger extended his hand through the window. The driver glanced briefly at the shining metal badge, and shifted to high.

VIII

Inspector Cramer's fifth telephone call to his office during the afternoon, made from a booth in a florist's shop a few doors down from Leo Kranz's art gallery, was put through a few minutes before the arrival at headquarters of the taxi bearing the man with the portfolio, and therefore there was some delay before the inspector learned of the superb success of the tactics he had suggested with regard to the new development—that development of which he had first heard at the time of his previous phone call, prior to his visit to the National Indian Museum. But in any event, since he was a methodical man, Cramer would probably have kept his appointment with Portia Tritt. He had determined to make the acquaintance of the principal persons involved among their own surroundings rather than in the menacing atmosphere of the office of the chief of the homicide squad, and it was his custom to lay out a program and stick to it.

Miss Tritt's apartment on the twelfth floor of Nyasset House, overlooking the East River, was a subtle triumph of her personality. It was expensively and elegantly trite, with its Ferinda mirror and photographic murals by Dickinson in the entrance hall, and in the living room, geometric rugs, bentwood furniture by Weber, copies of two Epsteins, and Diego Rivera sketches; but in spite of that it had the air and the feeling of a place where someone lived and wanted to live. Inspector Cramer, however, wasted no appreciation on the triumph; nor surprise on the luxury, for among the things which the reports had taught him about Portia Tritt was the fact that she was one of the eight or ten women whose varied activities in the New York fashion world were netting them incomes in excess of the salary of the President of the United States. Some things, of course, he had not been taught, as for instance that the Vionnet original of the afternoon dress she was wearing had sold for $800, whereas her copy by Nicholas had cost her nothing.

Cramer conjectured that her visible nervousness, as she recounted for him the story of her movements on the night of July 6th and the following morning, was probably habitual. In twenty minutes she took three cigarettes from a lacquered box, but never got one lit, she spoke hurriedly, and she sat her chair like a bird not on its chosen roost but on a momentary perch soon to be abandoned. Nevertheless, the story got told. She had ridden to Lucky Hills after lunch with Val Carew, driven by his chauffeur. Guy Carew had arrived that morning. There had been a long conversation between Guy and his father—not a quarrel, so far as she knew—and she and Guy had played a few sets of tennis. Later Buysse had come, and Leo Kranz, and the Barths. She knew nothing whatever of Barth's business with Carew, but a remark of Carew's had led her to suppose that Barth had phoned that morning to request an appointment, and that Carew was grimly amused that his wife was to accompany him. She had noticed nothing unusual in anyone's conduct before or during dinner, or after. After dinner she had played billiards with Kranz, and when Kranz went up a little after eleven she had decided to go for a walk.

Cramer put in, "Had you seen either of the Carews since dinner?"

"No."

"Did you see Guy when you went outdoors? He was on one of the terraces."

"I didn't go that way. It was a cool evening, and I went first to the side hall, to get a jacket from the closet, and then left by the main entrance, to tell Orson not to lock me out."

"Okay. Orson says it was 11:25 when you spoke to him. You came back in at one o'clock?"

"Around that, yes." Portia Tritt abandoned her fourth cigarette to a tray without having lit it. The tip of her tongue showed for an instant between her lips, and disappeared. She looked straight at the inspector. "Of course," she said, "I know that the decencies of privacy no longer exist—for that night—for any of us who were there. I realize you have to know everything, and anyway, you already do. You are aware that Mr. Carew and I intended to be married. You are aware of his habit of consulting—the sunlight on his dead wife's face, in her tomb. I suppose you are aware that he had not in fact engaged to marry me, that he had informed me that he intended to let the decision be made on that morning in his wife's tomb. . . ."

The tip of her tongue showed again. "But perhaps that isn't the way to say it. We had, really, agreed that we would marry. But he had let me understand that he couldn't fulfill the agreement without Tsianina's approval—or, as he said, her indifference. That sounds as if I had got myself into a humiliating position, and I had. Nobody could understand how it happened and my reason for submitting to it without knowing Val Carew and my reason, and I assure you we understood each other perfectly. But, why I say this, it was not only humiliating, it was ridiculous—it *is* ridiculous, my explanation of why I went outdoors and stayed until one o'clock. I wanted to look at the sky. I wanted to know if it seemed likely that the sun would be shining in the morning."

Cramer grunted. "It may have been ridiculous, but it was practical. And at one o'clock?"

"I went to my room. I didn't undress, because when I'm on edge I know I can't sleep, so I sat and tried to read. Perhaps I read some, but not much. At two o'clock—exactly that, for I looked at my watch—I reached a decision that I had been trying to make. I left my room and went to Guy Carew's room and knocked on his door, and he let me in."

She stopped. Cramer, with narrowed eyes on her, demanded, "Go on from there."

She shook her head. "That's all. Except that I stayed in his room, and he was with me, until half past seven, when Wilson came and said he had found—Val Carew's body."

Cramer, continuing to gaze at her, folded his arms and straightened his shoulders. Finally he sighed. "Look here, Miss Tritt. There were two things in particular I wanted to go over with you. This is one of them. You can't possibly get away with this. The police have been more than square with you. Not only has this not been published, it hasn't even been whispered. But sooner or later someone's going to be arrested and tried for murdering Val Carew, and the odds are a thousand to one you'll be on the witness stand. See what you think of the decencies of privacy then, when you are asked why you went to Guy Carew's room at two in the morning and stayed there for over five hours. If you refuse to say, there are only two possible surmises, or rather three. One is that you're lying. Another is that what you are concealing is guilty knowledge of the murder. The third you can guess—and Guy is the son of the man you expected to marry. I'm not accusing you of any of these motives for concealment; I'm just showing you the logic of it, and how that logic will work if you insist on giving it a chance, not among a few policemen, but with twelve people in a jury box and ten million people who read newspapers. You can't get away with it."

Portia Tritt said calmly, "The ten million—if it comes to that—may think what they please. As for a jury—what is there for a jury? Guy Carew is not a murderer. I am not."

"That may be a point at issue."

"Before a jury?"

"I say it may."

She shook her head. "That's a weaker threat, even, than the other. I'm not an ingénue, Inspector. Neither am I a holy terror. I'm thirty-three years old. For fifteen years I've wriggled through the mob, pinching and kicking and scratching and pulling hair, and—I'm where I am. The main trick is to keep all your own scars on the inside, where they don't show. You threaten me with odium." She laughed a little, not nicely. "You're much too late with that. Haven't you studied chemistry? Don't you know that the air we breathe is composed of nitrogen, oxygen and odium? No? All I have to say, I said that morning at Lucky Hills, when the air was also filled with fear and suspicion and suspense and policemen. I went to Guy Carew's room at two o'clock, and neither of us left there for five and a half hours."

Cramer blurted at her, "Did you have an affair with him in Paris in 1929?"

She countered, instantly, "What does he say?"

"He doesn't say."

"Then neither do I. I'm not a braggart."

"You knew him in Paris?"

"Yes, I met him."

"Did Val Carew know that you had known his son?"

"Yes."

"Did he know you had been intimate?"

"No more than you do."

"Did he learn of your former intimacy with his son on July 6th? Did Guy tell him about it that day? Is that what you went to Guy's room to talk about?"

"Three questions?" With a little smile Portia Tritt elevated her left hand to the level of her lips—admirable lips, neither too strong nor too dainty; with the index finger—a lovely, shapely finger—perpendicular. "No." The middle finger was erected beside its fellow. "No." The ring finger up. "No."

"Okay. How much have you seen of Guy Carew since 1929?"

"Nothing. Oh, perhaps a few casual meetings. Most of the time he has been out West. You know he has been doing things for the Indians?"

"So I understand. Have you had correspondence with him?"

"Never." She procured a cigarette from the lacquered box. "To tell the truth, I had forgotten his existence, until last summer, when Val Carew was introduced to me by my friend Leo Kranz. Then of course I remembered his son."

"And although you had forgotten his existence, you went to his room uninvited at two in the morning?"

"I did."

"And you are not telling why?"

"I am not."

"Do you suppose if the fact appeared in the newspapers it might remind somebody of something?"

"I wouldn't think so. I don't know who it could be, or what." She smiled. "It really couldn't help you, Inspector, neither the publication nor the threat of it. I told you I'm immunized to odium. Not that it's my favorite diet." She smiled again. "I appreciate your not publishing it—very much. And I shouldn't expect an official of your standing to publish it merely in order to get even with me for having zones of discretion. What I think is, I think it was pretty decent of me to admit that I had visited a man in his room and stayed most of the night—a man who would certainly never have revealed it himself—to save him from the possibility of a suspicion that he had murdered his father. I might have waited until the suspicion was a fact instead of a possibility."

"Yeah, so you might." Cramer folded his arms tighter, and sighed again. Suddenly he demanded, "What date was it that Carew took you inside the tomb and you left your fingerprints scattered around?"

"Sunday, July 4th." Her brows went up. "Good heavens, was that the second thing you wanted to go over with me? I suppose it is necessary for you to suspect everything anyone says, but there is corroboration for that. The Indian, Wilson, was there and saw us go in."

"The Indian don't remember it."

"Does he deny it?"

"He just can't remember it."

"Well." She upturned a palm. "He hates me, of course. I don't suppose he killed Val Carew, but he would have cheerfully killed me. But really, Inspector, you don't dream that I killed Val Carew myself, do you? If there is any significance to those fingerprints—"

She jerked up and around. The noise that had startled her—the ring of a telephone bell—seemed much too ordinary to have produced the effect it did; and Cramer's gaze concentrated on the back of her head as she stepped quickly across to a cabinet and pulled open a panel to disclose the instrument within. But if the sound of the bell had rudely disconcerted her, as it seemed to, she had her voice well composed as she spoke into the transmitter. In a moment she turned:

"It's for you, Inspector."

Cramer crossed to her, nodded thanks, and took it. His end of the conversation was not very informative, consisting mostly of grunts, with a few brief questions, and at one point an excited but vague ejaculation. At the end he said brusquely, "No. Hold everything. We've got to be absolutely sure. I'll be there as quick as I can make it."

He pushed the instrument back, turned, and was curt: "Much obliged, Miss Tritt. I have to go look at something. I'll be seeing you again—don't bother—I am used to opening doors—"

When he had gone, Portia Tritt stood staring at a deformed Epstein and as she did so succeeded, with completely mechanical movements, in getting a cigarette lit. After a dozen puffs she finally moved to an ash tray on a stand and deposited the matchstick and crushed the cigarette, went to the next room for a glance in the mirror, a hat and a cape which went with her dress, and got a handbag from a drawer. Before leaving the apartment she stopped at the outer door to take a look in the handbag.

Down on the sidewalk, the doorman leaped into action at sight of her. In the taxi, having given the driver an address, she looked through the back window; then, after a couple of blocks, again; and after three more blocks, once more. Her lips compressed with annoyance, and she spoke to her driver: "Go to the Hotel Churchill and stop in front of the shop marked Nicholas on the Fifty-fourth Street side." She didn't bother to look back again.

She had the change ready at the destination, paid the driver and hopped out and across the sidewalk to the door marked Nicholas. It was locked. She muttered, "Damn it, of course, I'm out of my mind," skipped into a tobacco shop next door, passed straight through it into the lobby of the Churchill, went on past palms and elevators and people into the arcade, another corridor and out to Fifty-third Street. There she stopped a taxi, got in, and told the driver to wait a minute. Looking through the rear window, she noted the cars and taxis crossing the avenue toward her, and those rounding the corner. After a moment she gave the driver an address and told him, "Get past Park on this light if you can make it."

She watched through the rear window, intermittently, until the taxi stopped at the curb on East Sixty-first Street.

She smiled through force of habit at the Japanese in a dark-blue uniform who let her in. That smile, which was no effort at all, had made ten thousand friends in ten thousand places where friendliness might never be needed, but should it be it was there.

"I'm expected, Nobu. I'm late."

"Yes, Miss Tritt. In the library—"

"All right, don't bother."

She turned to the staircase and went up, not rapidly, and down the wide second-floor hall to the door at the end. Before she reached it, it opened, and Leo Kranz was on the sill. She stopped, and their eyes met, and nothing was said; then he bowed and stepped aside and invited her, "Come in." She entered, and after he had closed the door he turned: "Your hat and gloves? Your cape?"

She shook her head, standing, glancing sharply around, and back at him. Then she shrugged, took off her hat and put it on a table, sat down with her handbag on her lap, and began pulling at her gloves.

"I apologize for being late," she said, "but I couldn't help it. I told you on the phone that police inspector was coming at 5:30, but he didn't get there until 6:00. Then he stayed longer than I thought he would. Then I didn't care to have the detective who follows me—damn it, Leo, don't look at me like that! You're not a dog! I don't like dogs."

"I know you don't. I beg your pardon." Kranz moved a chair and sat. "I knew the inspector would be late for his appointment with you because it was nearly 6:00 when he left my place."

"Oh! He called on you too?"

"Naturally. I was at Lucky Hills that night, so I am suspected of murder. I was one of Val's closest friends, so I am suspected of knowing things which I don't know. Inspector Cramer is the head of the homicide squad and was called back from a Canada vacation to solve the case."

Silence. It was prolonged. Portia Tritt put her gloves neatly together and thrust them under the strap of her handbag. She pulled her skirt down over her knee, dabbed at her nose with her handkerchief, clasped her hands on her lap, and unclasped them. Finally she inquired in a voice with a bare suggestion of tremor:

"Well?"

75

"Well?" Kranz smiled, not humorously. "You phoned that you wanted to come to see me. I confess I was surprised, considering the number of times I've asked you in the past month. . . ."

"Don't be suave, Leo. You know perfectly—" With an impatient gesture she jerked her handbag open, took a paper from it, and extended her hand. "What's that?"

He took it and looked at it. "It's an envelope, addressed to you, with my return printed on it—this address. In fact, it's one of my personal envelopes, and the inscription is my handwriting. Since it has no stamp, I presume it was delivered by messenger."

"Thanks. What's inside of it?"

He inserted two long deft fingers into the envelope, which had been slit open, and withdrew a fold of thin soft yellow material. It was so thin and soft he had difficulty unfolding it.

He held it by two corners: "Do you really want me to tell you what it is?"

"Please."

He shrugged. "It's a sheet of yellow Pasilex. Pasilex is the trade name of a luxury brand of paper handkerchief, used for wiping creams from the skin and similar purposes. It is superfine and so expensive that its distribution is limited to rich people—and to those who get it for nothing in publicity's name. I believe it comes in several colors; as I say, this one is yellow."

"Why did you send it to me?"

"Because I wanted to see you. Because for over two weeks you have avoided meeting me alone and refused to talk with me. Because it was vital that you *should* talk with me. Because you broke two promises to come, and I knew of no other way to get you here."

"Where did you get the idiotic notion that I would come if you sent me that?"

"Idiotic? Dear Portia! I sent it at three o'clock, when you didn't show up at the gallery. You are here, less than five hours later. And by the way, Nobu will have dinner—"

"No, thanks." Her eyes stayed level at him. "I want to know why you sent it."

He opened his hands. "To get you here."

"Damn it, Leo! Why did you send it?"

He looked at her. She met his gaze. In a moment he asked in a new tone, "You want to know why? Do you, Portia?" He stood up and took a step toward her eyes. "You know why. I had to see you. You know how desperately I love you. I have loved you for five years. I have had you for twenty-two months. I had, I know, I had only crumbs—but they were your crumbs—and no one else. At least I believed that—no one else—and I still believe it. You were honest with me about Val. I'm not a sentimental fool, I'm as good a realist as you are, Portia, and I took that, your decision to marry Val. I took it. You may say I had to take it, there was nothing I could do about it after my talk with him two months ago—but anyway, I took it—"

She moved, a jerk of impatience. "I don't need a history lecture. Why did you send me that sheet of Pasilex?"

"I'll get to it. The history is the prelude. I'm reminding you that I gave you up once. I won't again." He stopped; his lips worked; he controlled them. "I won't again, Portia. You're going to marry me, and that will settle it. I know how ambition burns in you, and I even respect it; it was proper and logical for you to become the mistress of one of the great American fortunes; but that ordeal is over for me and I won't submit to it again. You have been mine and now you are mine again. I wanted you before, because I loved you and because we suited each other—we fitted—we went together—" His hand fluttered. "Now I want you for that— and also because I find I must have you." His voice was suddenly harsh. "You've got inside of me—fatally—fatally, Portia!"

He stopped, gazing at her, and put out a hand and took it back again. "No," he said. "I'm not going to plead with you. I did that, and what good did it do? But all the same, I won't tolerate it—what you're doing with Guy Carew. Now that the fortune is his—the wings for your ambition. I know you can do it—he's a half-primitive infant—maybe you've already done it—but I won't tolerate it and I won't allow it. I won't, Portia! You're mine! By God, you are!"

Their gazes met. He was trembling. But soon, abruptly, he was still and controlled. He turned and sat down and looked at her with steady composure. His voice was smooth and firm: "That's why I sent you that sheet of yellow Pasilex. It came from a box which I bought. The nine sheets you used on July 6th are in my possession. I keep them for only one purpose: to show them to Guy Carew, and tell him how you used them, if it becomes necessary."

"I presume you're crazy." Her voice was as good as his. "If you think you know what you're talking about—"

"No, my dear." He shook his head. "It won't do. It's no good at all. I found it myself—where you put it. I know all about it. I even know you had a key for the tomb—I guessed that, first, because that was the only way you could have got in."

Portia Tritt sat and looked at him. She wet her lips. After a long silence she wet her lips again, and spoke. "You say you found it yourself? You got it yourself?"

He nodded.

"No one else knows about it? No one knows you have it?"

"No one."

"Then that explains . . ." A frown was creasing her forehead. "When did you find it? How did you get it? I don't see how you could possibly—"

She stopped, gaping at him; the blood left her face; horror was in her eyes. "Good God!" Her hands gripped the arms of the chair. "Good God, Leo! You killed Val!"

He shook his head.

"You did! You must have! There was no way . . . you could only . . ."

He shook his head again. "Portia dear. Please. Please! Listen to me. You know very well I couldn't have killed Val. It was quite simple. After Wilson came with the news, I went to the tomb with Guy. Guy left me there with Val's body—I was alone there ten minutes or more. I looked around, I went up the stone steps—and I saw it. I took a harpoon from the wall and got it. Naturally I wiped my fingerprints from the harpoon handle, since a man had been murdered there. I knew at once it was yours—who else in that house would have had yellow Pasilex? Anyway, it was obvious—the purpose. Later, thinking it over, it became equally obvious that you must have had a key, and I investigated. Discreetly."

He put out an appealing hand. "Don't narrow your eyes at me, Portia. Don't pretend that you think it possible that I murdered my old friend—even for you. And don't—you can't —blame me for using a weapon that fell into my hands. Better thank God it was me. What if the police had found it? They wouldn't have known at once, as I knew, that you use yellow Pasilex, but they certainly would have discovered it. My dear! I'm not holding the police over your head, I'm not holding anything over your head, I'm only saying that I love you and I must have you—and you won't force me to go to Guy Carew with this—"

"Bah!"

His brows lifted. "Bah?" he inquired.

"Yes, Leo. Bah. Guy wouldn't believe you."

"I think he would. I can offer corroboration—for instance, the key."

"Do you have a key?"

"No. You have."

"Then . . . a search warrant?"

"It wouldn't be necessary. Since I knew Val intimately, and all his habits—among others, the pocket on his belt in which he kept the key to the tomb—and since his valet, Richards, was therefore the only person who could have had an opportunity to take an impression of the key—do you think so simple a calculation was beyond me? You can't depend on Richards, Portia. Val is dead, and it's a case of murder. Guy can be made to believe. And Tsianina was his mother, and he loved her, and your trespass was in her tomb. Don't think, because people like you and me have abandoned reverence, that there is none left. What you did was desecration —what—"

He jumped up. "What the devil—"

Portia Tritt was on her feet, moving to the table, reaching for her hat and cape. She said calmly, "I'm going."

He grasped her arm. She shook loose and got her hat on. He stepped back, picked up the sheet of yellow Pasilex, and extended it in a hand not quite steady. "And this?" he demanded.

"I'll let you know." Her cape was around her shoulders.

"I prefer to know now."

"I'll let you know."

"But, Portia—I said I wouldn't plead with you again—but my God, you simply can't force me—"

"I'll let you know, Leo." She faced him, and by her straightness seemed almost as tall as he was. "I am fully capable of recognizing a rotten mess when I see one. I take back what I said about your murdering Val; you're not the type. One thing I'm afraid of, I'm afraid I don't like you much."

She moved swiftly to the door, through it, along the hall, down the broad stairs. Below, the Japanese, having heard her descent, came trotting and, seeing her accoutered with hat and cape, at once opened the outer door. As she passed through she said, "Thank you, Nobu," and smiled at him.

IX

Jean Farris would probably not have been guilty of trite elegance in her home even if she had been able to afford it; but the question is academic and therefore not worth enlarging upon, for she couldn't afford it. She had finally, after a protracted struggle, matured her talent for design and found successful application for it; but so far, all the profits had been carefully funneled into the bottle for nursing the infant business. So, in the modest three rooms she rented in the Fifties near Lexington Avenue, her bed was merely a bed and her chairs merely something to sit on. Its charm, if you liked it, was due to the circumstance that the draperies, rugs and upholstery were in fabrics of her own design.

Friday evening at eight o'clock she was there, alone at the little table in the living room eating a strawberry tart, and thanking heaven for Oletha, who had cooked the tart as well as the dish of spaghetti with mushrooms, tomatoes and chicken livers which had preceded it. Having left her office before five for a necessary visit to the workshop of Muir & Beebe, and having begged off from a dinner engagement with Adele Worthy of *Harvey's Bazaar* on account of a combined buzz and ache in her head, she was now enjoying the taste of the tart and the smell of the black coffee, and looking forward to a leisurely cigarette, a still more leisurely warm bath, and a clean white bed with a soft pillow for her abused head.

The doorbell rang, and she called, "Punch it, will you, Oletha?" She didn't know why she always did that, since Oletha would of course have punched it anyway, unless it was because she liked to hear the soft voice calling from the little kitchen, "Yes, Miss Jean!" She took the penultimate bite of tart. It was Friday; it would be the laundry; they came at all hours.

But after the wait for the caller to climb the two flights, and the opening of the hall door, and a brief murmur of voices, Oletha appeared and had her company manners on to announce, "A gentleman, Miss Jean—"

She was interrupted by the entrance of the gentleman himself, bulky, broad-shouldered, middle-aged at least, with a straw hat in his hand. Passing, he growled, "Thank you, Jemima," and approached the table. "I beg your pardon. Are you Miss Jean Farris? I'm Inspector Cramer of the homicide squad. Police inspector."

Jean's first feeling was hot resentment of the "Jemima." For one thing, she disliked vulgar familiarity, and for another, she thought Oletha was a lovely name. She was about to blurt something when she realized what else he had said. She hesitated, and then proceeded to blurt anyway:

"Do you walk in on people like this because you're an inspector? Or can any policeman do that?"

The caller grunted. "We walk in because if we don't sometimes we don't get in at all. Politeness is like a stick, it has two ends, and we only have hold of one. I begged your pardon. I do so again. Are you Miss Jean Farris?"

"I am."

"Then I need to have a talk with you."

"I hope . . ." Jean shrugged. "Bring the coffee, will you, Oletha?"

Oletha went. The caller observed, "I might as well sit down."

"Do so. That other chair is more comfortable."

He sat, deposited his hat on the floor beside him, crossed his ankles, and aimed a straight gaze at her. He declared as if he meant it, "I'm sorry to interrupt your meal, but this is urgent. I want to ask you something about a suit —a skirt and jacket—you wore yesterday afternoon."

Jean, with the last bite of tart in her mouth, stopped chewing for an instant. Then her jaws moved again. She waited until she had swallowed before inquiring, "Yes? What about it?"

"You wore it yesterday afternoon to Melville Barth's place up near Portchester. There was a lot of talk about it. Around 8:15 you disappeared. At dinnertime, nine o'clock, they couldn't find you, and decided you had run out on them. A little before ten you showed up at the house minus the suit and said someone had hit you on the head and took it. Right?"

Jean said, "Thanks, Oletha. Leave the pot, please. You go whenever you're through." She put in a lump of sugar and began stirring, then looked aside at the inspector. "I didn't complain to the police, did I?"

"No, ma'am, you didn't."

"Then how did you—Oh!" She turned, her eyes open at him. "You've found it!"

"No, ma'am, we haven't found it. Not so far as I know. As to how we learned about it, there were twenty people at that dinner table, and when there's talk about an incident like that we're apt to hear of it sooner or later, especially when seven of the persons present are more or less involved in a murder case. But I'd like to have you confirm it. Did it happen that way?"

Jean nodded. "Approximately. Except the way you told it—you said I *said* someone hit me on the head. Someone *did* hit me on the head."

"And took your suit?"

"Presumably. I was unconscious. To assume that the per-

81

son who hit me was the one who took the suit—it seems plausible."

"Yeah. Have you any idea who did it?"

"Not the slightest."

"Or why it was done?"

"No. My watch and ring and purse weren't taken."

"Yeah. What he wanted was the suit. Was that the first time you ever wore that suit, Miss Farris?"

"Yes."

"Who made it for you?"

Jean took a sip of coffee. Her head was buzzing, and she was feeling that it was particularly desirable that at this moment her head should be clear. She took another sip, and another. Then she turned and tried a smile:

"Really, Inspector, I don't quite see why I should discuss this affair with you. I haven't requested your help, have I? And besides, aren't you a New York inspector? This didn't happen in the city, it was in Westchester County."

Cramer grinned. "Don't worry about the jurisdiction part. That's all right. New York and Westchester—we're all one big family. As for discussing it, why should you object?" He spread out his hands. "What I'm asking you is no secret —like who made it for you. Isn't that more or less common knowledge? I just want to be sure a few facts are correct, and you're the best one to ask, if you don't mind."

Common knowledge? Yes, Jean thought, of course. She said, "Krone made it. Krone, West Forty-eighth Street."

"Thanks. And you furnished the material?"

"Yes."

"Your own design?"

"Yes."

"Did you weave it yourself?"

"Yes."

"On a loom in your own shop?"

"Yes."

"With yarn?"

"Certainly. One weaves with yarn."

"Yeah. Was some of the yarn that you used a kind called bayeta?"

Jean's mouth opened, and closed again. Unquestionably, she needed a clear head and didn't have it. She lifted her coffee cup and half emptied it, scalding her throat. She grabbed her glass of water and took a mouthful, and swallowed.

She looked at the inspector: "I'll tell you. Frankly. I've decided not to say anything more about it."

"But we're nearly to the end, Miss Farris. Practically there. As for the bayeta, didn't you announce it yesterday yourself, publicly, to various people? Didn't you?"

"Yes."

"It was bayeta, wasn't it?"

"Yes."

"Okay. There's only one more question, and after that maybe a couple of details, and that's all. Where did you get the bayeta yarn?"

Jean's fingers tightened on the handle of the coffee cup. Of course. Here it was. Here she was. He had certainly got to the point in a hurry. With a clear head, could she have kept him away from it? But what the devil, after all, it was simple. That you were asked for a fact didn't mean that you must surrender it; and it wasn't like a skirt and jacket; they couldn't knock you on the head and strip you of it. She turned to him:

"Now you are after a secret, Inspector. I can't tell you where I got the yarn."

"Why can't you tell?"

"Because . . ." Then Jean thought her head must be clearing, because a brilliant idea popped into it. "Because I've forgotten."

Cramer grunted. "Oh, my God. When did you get it?"

"I don't know. I've forgotten."

"Nonsense. I happen to know that you got it within the past month. Where did you get it?"

"Really, Inspector, I don't remember."

He sat and gazed at her in silence, frowning, his eyes now absolutely unfriendly. Finally he sighed, got up, and walked across to confront her. "Look here, Miss Farris. Get this. I haven't got time to fool around. I don't know whether you know what kind of a mess you've stepped into or not. It's barely possible you think you're just playing bean bag, but you're not. This is a different kind of a game entirely. Either you tell me within, say three minutes, where you got that bayeta yarn, or you're on your way to headquarters under arrest."

Jean was so shocked and incredulous that she even wanted to laugh, but somehow didn't. She merely stared, and demanded weakly, "Arrest? What for?"

"As a material witness in the Valentine Carew murder case."

The growl of a lioness defending her cub came from the door to the kitchen. That was Oletha.

X

Neither paid any attention to Oletha's growl. Jean continued to stare, with her chin tilted up. Her head had suddenly stopped buzzing and felt clear and cool. So it wasn't simple after all; apparently far from it.

She said, "Sit down again, please."

"There's no use sitting down unless you're going to tell me where you got that yarn. We might as well be going."

"I wish you *would* sit down."

Cramer glared a moment, then returned to his chair. "All right. Shoot."

"First—I want to ask—I don't know much about the law—can you arrest somebody you want to like this—when they haven't done anything?"

"We can."

"And actually *take* them—to jail?"

"Yes. It is lawful to arrest anyone who is in possession of vital evidence in a capital crime and refuses to divulge it."

"Oh." Jean's stare was now only a level regard. "What makes you think I have vital evidence?"

"I don't think. I know all about it." Cramer leaned forward. "Listen here, Miss Farris. You don't want any part of this. The best thing you can do is unload completely. I'll be frank. I have no idea what else you know or don't know, or did do or didn't do, but I know damn well you know where you got that yarn. That detail is sewed up. It won't do any harm to give you a clear idea of where you stand; maybe that will show you how foolish it is for you to try to hold out. You may know, or you may not, that when Valentine Carew was found murdered he held clutched in his hand a strand of bayeta yarn which he had obviously torn from the clothing of the murderer. Under a microscope that yarn has been compared with fifty or more samples of bayeta taken from various places. Two hours ago it was discovered that it is identical with the bayeta yarn you used in weaving your suit. That's why I say you have vital evidence in a capital crime. We've got to know where you got the yarn, and we're going to know."

"But you have no evidence." Jean was calm. "You can't possibly know the two yarns are identical. How could you, without a sample of mine?"

"We couldn't. We've got the sample."

"Of the yarn I used? You— Oh! You have found the suit!"

"Not the suit. We have a strand of the yarn you used, taken from your own file, with a signed statement to authenticate it."

"Signed by whom?"

"By the person we got it from. Eileen Delaney."

"Eileen—" Jean straightened and her eyes flashed. "That's a lie!"

"No, ma'am. It's the truth. She's all right, she'll explain it—we don't want to bust up a partnership." He gestured impatiently. "Forget it, that can wait. I'm just letting you know where you stand. If you don't tell me where you got that yarn, two things can happen to you. First, I can take you down as a material witness, and keep you, and I'm going to, and we'll even fight bail if I have anything to say. Second, there's a chance that you'll be prosecuted as an accessory to murder. That's not a threat, it's information. You asked about the law, and I'm telling you. I'm also telling you, as a man of experience, that you're acting like a lunatic. You can't possibly have any stake in this that's worth what it would cost you. You never knew Val Carew, and you never met his son until two weeks ago. You never knew Buysse or that Indian. You only had a casual acquaintance with the Barths. You only had business relations with Portia Tritt, and not even business relations with Leo Kranz. So as I say, your ante in this game can't be anything big, and you're a plain lunatic if you don't cash in and exit. This is not—where you going?"

Jean was swiftly crossing the room. Disregarding his question, she reached the stand in the corner which held the telephone, and rapidly and accurately, in spite of her trembling hand, started to dial. But the inspector was rapid too. He was across to her as the dial was whirring for the first digit, and his big hand was heavy on dial and cradle both.

He shook his head and said calmly, "No, ma'am."

Jean tugged an instant, gave up, jerked her hand away, and stood with blazing eyes. "That's my telephone!"

"Not right now it ain't. Right now nothing's yours. I've been trying to tell you, in a murder case it's a new set of rules entirely. I know what they are and you don't."

Jean wheeled and called, "Oletha!"

"Yes, Miss Jean?"

"Run down to the corner and phone Miss Delaney and tell her to come here at once—I don't suppose Oletha is under arrest too?"

Cramer shrugged. "Not interested in Oletha. But by the time your partner gets here you'll be gone. You can phone yourself from headquarters, one call—"

"Wait, Oletha." Jean's hands, at her sides, were tight fists. Her voice was tight too: "I suppose what you're doing is legal or you wouldn't do it. But even if I'm an accessory to a murder, which I'm not, is there any reason I shouldn't talk to my business partner? I want to tell her—there are things to be done at my office tomorrow—"

"Not tomorrow. Not by your partner." Cramer looked exasperated. "Don't you realize what's going on? Don't you think we already know that Krone made that suit, and we've talked to Krone and learned that he sent the scraps to you, by your order, in the same box the suit was delivered in? There are two men outside your place of business right now. Tomorrow morning there will be more, with a search warrant. We want those scraps of material, and we also want the rest of that bayeta yarn in your files."

"You'll search—" Jean's eyes were blazing again. "My office! You'll go through my files! My things! *Damn* you!"

Cramer shrugged. "I've been trying to tell you. Where did you get that yarn, Miss Farris?"

Jean stood and looked at him, without breathing. At length her frantic and indignant lungs made a peremptory demand which resulted in a convulsion of her chest as the air rushed in. She paid no attention to it. There were three more inhalations, the last one steady and deep, before she spoke in a firm controlled voice:

"All right. Excuse me for yelling at you. I suppose you like to do work you have a talent for, the same as I do. I hope —I've never been in a jail—am I allowed to take along some things? Toilet things and something to sleep in?"

"You can send for 'em later." It was a growl. "You won't be needing anything to sleep in tonight. Do you actually mean you're going to let me take you down?"

"What else can I do?"

"Goddam it, you can answer a plain simple question!"

"No. Really I can't. Oletha, will you phone Miss Delaney after I've gone? Tell her what's happened—and tell her to be at the office early tomorrow morning and try to keep them from tearing the place to pieces. And tell her—no. I suppose I should have a lawyer. Phone Mr. Raleigh, R,A,L,E,I,G,H. Timothy Raleigh, Cedar Street. There's no use trying to get him tonight; phone to his office in the morning. If a letter comes . . ."

Cramer, at the phone, had dialed a number and was talking: "Burke? Cramer. I'll be down there in about twenty minutes with Jean Farris. Have some men at the side door to cover her if there are any newshounds around, and watch your trap. Phone the commissioner and the D.A. and tell them it looks tough and they may want to sit in. Got that warrant?—Okay. Not tonight, morning will do. Don't forget the side door."

He hung up. He scowled at Jean Farris. "So," he said, "you're really tough, huh?"

"No, I'm not tough." Jean was calmly putting on her hat, but grimaced as she pulled it down on the left side. "Unless you mean stubborn. I'm stubborn enough. Come on."

XI

At 10:00 P.M., Eileen Delaney, on the phone, to Timothy Raleigh: "If you'll give me a chance I'll tell you. I'm not sure exactly where she is. The colored maid heard him say he was taking her to Police Headquarters. That's where I am now, talking from a booth. In another ten minutes I'll begin shooting everybody in sight, I swear to God I will. They won't let me see Inspector Cramer, or anyone else who amounts to anything. They won't tell me definitely whether she's here or not, but she must be. . . . I told you what the maid said, material witness in the Valentine Carew murder case, and Jean had as much to do with that as the man in the moon. She never saw Carew, she met his son about two weeks ago. . . . How the hell do I know? Then that business about the yarn, I haven't the slightest idea what it means. I mean I don't know what it means about murder. All I know is, you have to get busy and get her out. . . . Damn it, I'm perfectly aware it's night! Does the law die at sundown? Are you a lawyer? Did you ever hear of bail or habeas corpus or civil rights? If you want to talk to the maid, you can get her at Jean's apartment, I told her to stay there. I'm going to camp right here. . . ."

At 10:20 P.M., Eileen Delaney, on the phone, to Adele Worthy: "But, Adele, it's ridiculous, it's insane! Jean Farris is as apt to be mixed up in a murder as Albert Einstein! Of course it's a mistake, but how am I going to get her out of it if they won't even let me see her or tell me where she is? I've phoned three lawyers, and they say they'll see what they can do, but the poor saps seem to be afraid of the dark.

. . . No, I know you can't, but you know everybody in town, and surely you can gather enough pull to arrange for them to let me see her, at least. Do you realize they've got her somewhere and *nobody* knows where she is? Good God, it sounds like the Middle Ages! You do what you can, and I'll call again in half an hour, I'm going to stick here. . . ."

At 10:40 P.M., Adele Worthy, on the phone, to Portia Tritt: "It is terrible, it certainly is. Of course the publicity won't hurt her any if she comes out of it clean, I'll bet Ethel Gannon will be working overtime. I can just see her. But we do all love Jean, I know I do, and I phoned two men who may be able to do something, though nobody can get very far in a murder case, and it occurred to me that you used to know Bob Skinner before he became district attorney, and of course he's the one to reach. Maybe if you would phone him, or even see him, and use your corkscrew voice on him—no offense, Portia dear, but many's the time and oft you've used it to pull a page in the *Bazaar* out of me. . . ."

At 11:00 P.M., Adele Worthy, on the phone, to a man: "I'm sorry you couldn't get me, Art; the line's been busy and I guess it will be until midnight. I'm trying to rescue a damsel in distress. Jean Farris—you know, the designer—has been arrested and is being held at headquarters in connection with the Carew murder case. Some goofy tale about some yarn she used in her weaving— Oh, Lord, I forgot you work for a newspaper, I never think of you as a newspaperman because you're always so well-dressed and your hair is always combed—but I suppose your colleagues have already got it anyhow. . . ."

At midnight, Sergeant Burke, thoroughly exasperated, to the face of Eileen Delaney: "Damn it, I tell you she's not *in* jail! She's engaged with the commissioner and the district attorney! Certainly, you can stay here all week if you want to, and what good will that do you? What do you think, they're using a rubber hose on her? Piffle! The best thing you can do is go home and go to bed, and let your lawyers get some sleep too. . . ."

At 2:00 A.M., District Attorney Skinner, in a tired voice, to Jean Farris: "I think that's farfetched, to call it torture. We're only trying to get something it is our right and our duty to get. We're doing what the people of New York City hired us to do."

Commissioner Humbert was there too, but they were not upstairs in his spacious and comfortable office. It was Room Nine in the basement—a medium-sized room bare of all furniture but a wooden table, a dozen wooden chairs, and a built-in cupboard. That room had in fact witnessed on occasion employment of the cruder forms of the third degree, but of course not by officials of the eminence of those now present. Humbert, in a gray sack suit, with his hair rumpled, walked slowly up and down, frowning, smoking a cigarette. Skinner, in tails and the proper white tie, having come at midnight from a hotel roof, straddled one of the chairs bassackwards, with his arms crossed along its back. In another chair facing him was Jean, keeping herself upright with an effort, her hat off and her hair messy, with a bright light shining in her eyes. On Skinner's side it was shaded.

She had tried different tactics during the five hours she had been there. From 9:00 till 10:30, with Inspector Cramer and two men in uniform, she had replied, had discussed and even argued, on any subject that was far enough removed from the fact she would not disclose. But she found that was dangerous. Once—she could no longer remember how—she had nearly been trapped. With the arrival of Commissioner Humbert, who had blustered and glared at her with his face not more than twelve inches from hers, she had decided to try silence, to refuse to speak at all; simply to keep her mouth shut. At the end of thirty minutes she was amazed to find how difficult it was. Another half hour and she was clutching the edges of her chair seat to keep from screaming. The antics of Commissioner Humbert and the indignant strutting of his demands could be borne; but Cramer's calm unceasing persistence, his patient repetition of the same question a dozen, two dozen times, his trick of compelling her gaze by stopping abruptly in the middle of a sentence, and then, when she looked at him, quietly continuing—she felt she couldn't bear it much longer. She would find that she had involuntarily clapped her hand to her mouth and would pull it away, back to the edge of her chair. The light in her eyes was intolerable. She tried closing them, but would get dizzy and have to open them again. Cramer's calm voice went on inexorably; the questions he repeated oftenest were the most trivial ones, as for instance, "Was the bayeta yarn in the warp or the woof?" After the twentieth repetition of that the desire to shout "Woof!" and be rid of it was so irresistible that she had to sink her teeth into her lip; she mustn't; she had decided not to speak.

It was close to midnight, though she didn't know it, when she was suddenly dazed with panic at the realization that someone had clubbed her on the head, again and she had crashed. Things were blurred; she was being held by strong arms in a firm unyielding grasp; she struggled and strained. She became aware of Cramer's hateful voice:

"Now hold it. I'm just putting you back in the chair."

So he was. She felt it under her, and found that she had been released. She blinked up at him and demanded, "What happened? Someone hit me—"

"No, they didn't. Don't get that idea in your head, Miss Farris. You kept your eyes closed too long and fell off, and I didn't quite keep you from hitting the floor. Want a drink of water? Or maybe some coffee?"

"No, thank you."

"Okay. I was just asking, how many different kinds of yarn did you use in that material besides the bayeta?"

Jean remembered that she wasn't speaking.

A little later District Attorney Skinner arrived and was politely introduced. Soon after that, Jean felt a surge of relief when she saw that Cramer was departing. Skinner might be difficult, but he couldn't possibly be as bad as Cramer. She decided to abandon her policy of silence; she would go crazy if she tried to keep that up all night. She wished that she had accepted the offer of coffee, but she wouldn't ask for it. She would answer all harmless questions, but slowly, after thinking them over.

Among New York lawyers, District Attorney Skinner was generally considered to be one of the three cleverest cross-examiners in the city.

At two o'clock, her eyes burning, her head buzzing intolerably, and her fingers aching from their desperate grip on the edges of her chair seat, Jean told him she was being tortured. He said he thought that was farfetched and went on, "You say that because right now your values are all distorted. Naturally. You have to look at it with common sense. What are we actually doing to you? Keeping you up all night, that's all. Lots of people stay up all night fairly frequently without any compulsion; I expect you've done it yourself occasionally. It's the compulsion that makes you call it torture, and that's why I say it's farfetched."

His voice was calm and not high-pitched, but had a rasp in it which was like a steel rake on Jean's raw nerves. He went on, "We're as much under compulsion as you are; you should be intelligent enough to see that. We can't possiby let up on you, and we're not going to. We're mighty careful about taking unwarranted liberties with respectable citizens of good standing and good connections. We wouldn't be doing this if all we had on you was some sort of vague suspicion. You don't seem to realize what we do have on you. It's the same, for instance, as if Carew had been shot, and we found the gun that shot him in your possession, and you refused to tell where you got it. The fact that the yarn you used is identical with the piece found in Carew's hand is an absolutely definite link with the murderer, and it has got to be traced. That's our compulsion. Aside from the fact that we are the agents of justice, Carew was a millionaire, killed in a sensational manner under bizarre circumstances. More than a month ago. We've got nowhere, and the press and the public are howling at us. Now we get—open your eyes! Miss Farris! Open your eyes! Open your eyes! Open—"

She dragged them open.

"Now we get a direct trail to the murderer, and you try to keep it blocked. We can't possibly let up on you, and we're not going to let you go. With the evidence we have, nothing any lawyer can do will get you out. I'll be here with you until six o'clock. Inspector Cramer is taking a nap, and at that time he'll return and go on with it. Sooner or later, of course, you'll fall asleep, and a matron will put you to bed. We'll let you sleep a couple of hours and then wake you up and give you something to eat and resume. It will go on that way."

Skinner, frowning, pulled at the lobe of his ear and gazed at her. Abruptly he demanded, "Where did you get that yarn, Miss Farris?"

Jean said in a thin and querulous tone, "You might as well let up on me. I don't care if it goes on this way forever."

"You will though," Skinner rasped. "You've got a surprise coming. I've told you before, and I tell you again frankly, I don't think your emotions are enough involved for you to hold out. You're a woman. You're just trying to shoot square with someone, and that's not strong enough for a woman. It may be now, but wait until twelve hours from now, or twenty-four. It would be different if a deep emotion were concerned; for instance, if you were shielding a brother or a father or a man you're in love with. If it is something like that, as I told you, we will let up. In that case, I think you have enough stamina to beat us. We don't want to waste our time. It can't be a brother or a father. Is it a man you love, Miss Farris?"

Jean strained to keep her eyes open. Questions like that were dangerous; she had a dim recollection that he had almost caught her, long ago, by starting on that line. She let her eyes close and then strained them open again, and told him, "There's no use trying that again. I won't answer anything like that."

XII

In a large room on the 32nd floor of a Madison Avenue building in the Forties, Samuel Aaron Orlik sat at his desk, his arms folded and lips screwed up, staring at the knob of the door twenty feet away. The room was beautifully furnished, in excellent and quiet taste. The polished and spacious top of the desk was bare except for an onyx pen stand, an empty letter basket, a crystal glass ash tray, and a morning newspaper which displayed a prominent headline:

ARREST IN CAREW MURDER CASE

Orlik moved his right forearm sufficiently to expose the watch on his left wrist: ten after nine. He grunted impatiently, and at that moment there was a soft buzz and he swiveled to reach the phone on its bracket. In a moment he said, "Well, I told you to send him in, didn't I?" Then he got up and went to the door and opened it. He shook hands with the tall dark young man who presently came down the hall, allowed him precedence in entering and, back in the room, closed the door.

The visitor said in a tone of displeasure, "This is a waste of time, my stopping here. We could have met downtown. I told you on the phone—"

"Please, Mr. Carew. Have a seat." Orlik himself sat. "Now, you might as well sit down. This has to be discussed."

"I don't see why." Guy Carew remained standing. "You know as much about it as I do. I told you everything yesterday when I gave you that piece of yarn I got from Miss Farris. They've got onto it somehow, I don't know how, and it doesn't matter. The only thing that matters is to get down there and make them turn her loose. My God, she's been there all night! I didn't know about it until I saw the paper—"

"I did. I knew at midnight."

"What?" Guy stared.

"I said I learned of it at midnight. I know lots of people who are glad to tell me things." Orlik folded his arms. "You confounded millionaires! When Hutchings & Osborn asked me to take this I was inclined to turn it down. I hate millionaires for clients; I'd rather have one who has to mortgage his home and borrow on his insurance to pay me; they expect less and they appreciate more. But I'm giving you my very best—"

"Not sitting there, you're not. You've already delayed it an hour."

"And I'm going to delay it ten minutes more to tell you something. Granting that I'm the best criminal lawyer on feet, do you think I can run down to Centre Street and snap my fingers and all the doors will fly open? Look here, Mr. Carew. I'm presuming that you've told me the truth, and the whole truth, about everything, including that jacket and the yarn that was in it. If that is so, there is no way in God's world to get that young woman away from the police until they either learn what they want to know or become convinced they can't get it out of her, and it will take some convincing. I heard of it at midnight, and I've been working on it, and it looks certain that somehow they've got hold of a piece of that yarn and compared it with their piece. Nothing else would account for the way they're handling it; they wouldn't dare; Cramer might have taken her down on suspicion, because he really has guts, but Skinner would have got cold feet when the lawyers began to show up, as they did before midnight. Also that Delaney woman nearly tore the building apart. I've had several reports from friends of mine. And no one has even been allowed to have a glimpse of her. That means Skinner's sitting tight, and when he's sitting tight he's sitting pretty."

Orlik unfolded his arms, leaned forward, and elevated his chin to look up. "I only hope to God she has enough sense and guts to keep her mouth shut. One of those lawyers is pretty good, a fellow named Raleigh, and they'll have to let him see her this morning and he'll buck her up. You say go down there and get her out? I can't even go, let alone get her out. The minute I put in a peep for her, we might as well make a signed statement that you gave her the jacket, since they know I'm your lawyer."

"All right." Guy still stood. "We'll make a statement. Anything. I can't let her—I tell you she's been there all night—"

"My God!" Orlik spread out his hands. "She had to spend the night somewhere. They're not hurting her any. That would be fine, to admit you gave her the jacket, with the story that the last you saw of it was when you put it in the closet Tuesday afternoon, and the next you saw of it was two weeks later in your own room. As I say, I'm accepting your story, Mr. Carew. I'm accepting a good deal. I know I'm not defending you against a charge of murder, and I'm not likely to be, with the alibi you have. But let them once learn that that piece of yarn came from your jacket, and they'll be like the mule—blind on one side of the face and can't see out of the other. As I've said before, they're either going to solve it or they're not. If they don't, you say you want me to solve it. In that case, I must be handicapped as little as possible. I certainly don't want to have—"

"That can wait," Guy snapped impatiently. "Certainly I want you to solve it, but you haven't done it yet, and I guess it can wait while we get Miss Farris released. Right this minute that's all I'm interested in. I realize that it's preferable to do it by a process of law; that's why I phoned you and that's why I stopped here when you insisted. You're my lawyer and I'm paying you. Are you going to do it?"

"You mean this morning? Today?"

"I mean now."

"I can't." Orlik spread out his hands again. "Haven't I been telling you? Damn it, I don't dare appear for her. They won't hurt her. If she's willing to stand the gaff—hey! Mr. Carew!"

Guy, striding toward the door, paid no attention. He turned the knob and pulled, and passed through. He was ten paces down the hall when he heard trotting footsteps behind him and a voice low but tense with fury: "You go down there and make a fool of us and I warn you, I throw it up! I'm out! I'm your attorney and you've got to take—"

Guy, without slackening, told him calmly, "All right, get out and go to hell." He reached the outer door, let himself through, walked along the public corridor to the elevators, took a down car, pushed rudely ahead of others at the main floor, went to the street, found a taxi at the curb, gave the driver an address, and hopped in and sat on the edge of the seat. To a Cherokee his face might have suggested a thunderbird mask in a corn dance.

At a quarter to ten Jean Farris had no idea whether it was eight in the morning or six in the afternoon. If she had been wasting energy on hope, her hope would have been that it was afternoon, on the ground that the more time there is behind you the less there is in front. History was vague and even unimportant. She knew, or rather, supposed, that some time around dawn she had collapsed and been carried to bed; at least, she had at some hour or other found herself lying under a cotton blanket on a couch with her shoes off, after being coerced somewhat roughly into life by a large woman in a blue uniform who kept sneezing in her face. She had eaten part of something they brought her on a tray and swallowed two cups of surprisingly good coffee, and had been escorted back to the room in the basement by a man in uniform who refused to speak to her. In a few minutes Inspector Cramer appeared and proceeded to complete the process of waking her up, though of course not by touching her. It was really hate that woke her, hatred of his voice, which was like a prolonged nightmare persisting after sleep had been torn away.

"Feel a little better, Miss Farris? You had a good nap, nearly two hours. I want to ask you . . ."

Respite finally came—morning, afternoon, she didn't know, for they had refused to tell her the time—when the door opened and a man entered, three paces in, and beckoned to the inspector. Cramer went out with him, after saying something to a policeman who was on a chair over by the wall. The policeman got up and strolled to the chair Cramer had vacated, but remained standing and said nothing. Though she couldn't see very well with the light in her eyes and his in shadow, it seemed to Jean that he had a decent and friendly face, and she asked, "What time is it?"

He shook his head. "Sorry, miss." Then he glanced around at the door and, keeping his head turned that way, suddenly thrust out his left arm to its full extent, displaying a wrist watch. Jean peered and made it out: ten minutes to ten. She said, "Thanks." He looked up at the ceiling and murmured barely audibly, "Don't mention it."

In the hall, outside the door, Inspector Cramer was being presented with a problem. The man who had come for him had told him succinctly, "Guy Carew's here asking to see Jean Farris."

Cramer's eyes widened. "Where?"

"A reporter spotted him in the hall—Allen of the *Gazette*—and jumped for his throat. You know that baby. So I took him upstairs to your office. Burke's got him."

"What does he say?"

"He just says he understands Miss Farris is here and he wants to see her."

"Did you tell him she's here?"

The man looked pained. "No, sir. I made him spell her name."

"I'll be damned." Cramer gazed at the tip of the man's nose for a full minute. "Is the commissioner here?"

"No, sir."

"God Almighty. Maybe it's going to bust. Wait a minute,

let me think." Slowly he pulled out a cigar, stuck it into his mouth nearly to its middle, and clamped his teeth on it. He elevated his chin, and slowly and devastatingly chewed. "No good," he muttered. After he had chewed for two minutes he removed the cigar and hurled it down the hall, and said with decision: "Send a man in to keep Bingham company with Miss Farris. We don't want any solos on this case. I'll see Carew upstairs. You go up and wait with Burke. If I send for Miss Farris, don't call in the photographers."

He swung off down the dingy hall, turned a corner at the far end, and rang for an elevator. The elevator man saw the scowl on his face and stiffened to a more military posture. Getting off at the third floor and entering, down the hall, a door marked "Homicide Bureau," he strode through the anteroom without glancing aside and past a series of doors in a partition until at the end he opened one. It was a medium-sized room, innocent of luxury, with three windows, an old well-scarred desk, and chairs with faded leather seats. Cramer sat at the desk and pulled the telephone across, and in a moment told the transmitter, "Send Mr. Carew in here."

The door opened and Sergeant Burke appeared, following the knob in. The visitor passed through, and Burke went out again with the knob. Cramer stood up and extended a hand across the desk.

"How do you do, Mr. Carew. I'm Inspector Cramer."

"I beg your pardon." Guy stood four feet short of the desk. "I suppose I have no right to act like an Indian, since I've accepted the white man's money and clothes and education, but certain things—I'm sorry. I only shake hands with friends."

Cramer grunted. "Okay. Suit yourself. Have a seat. I understand you want to see Miss Jean Farris."

"Yes. I do."

"What makes you think she is here?"

"The newspapers. You arrested her. She is here. Isn't she?"

Cramer nodded. "Yeah, she's here. Been here all night. What do you want to see her about?"

Guy had stepped forward with a gleam in his eye and a muttered exclamation. "Oh, you admit—"

"I don't admit anything. I just say Miss Farris is here. What do you want to see her about?"

"I want to see her. I demand it as the right of a friend. She has committed no crime. It's not legal—"

"Now wait a minute, Mr. Carew. Let's leave it to the

lawyers what's legal. You're not a lawyer, are you? You're a citizen and I'm a cop. Let's take it easy. You say you want to see Miss Farris, and I say okay. Certainly you can see her."

Guy stared at him suspiciously. Paying no attention to that, he sat again, pulled the phone across, and spoke into it: "Burke? Is Stebbins there? Tell him to go down and get Miss Farris and bring her in here. Right away." He returned the instrument to its cradle. "You might as well sit down, Mr. Carew. She'll be here in a minute."

"Thanks." Guy turned to face the door and remained standing. He was directly between the desk and the door, and Cramer pushed his chair to one side on its casters to have an unobstructed view. Then he sat and regarded the back of Guy's head, with his lips compressed and his eyes steadily speculative. He could see Guy's shoulders lift and fall with breathing, and counted twenty-eight respirations in a minute. He opened his mouth to speak, then decided not to, and the silence continued.

The door opened. Stebbins' technique differed from that of Burke; he flung the door ahead of him and permitted the visitor to enter first. Jean came in two steps, with the light of the windows against her, and then stopped dead. Cramer was half out of his chair, to see better. Disheveled and pale as she was, the swift color showed in her cheeks, almost startlingly. "Guy!" she gasped. Then, suddenly aware of the inspector stretching his neck and staring, she jerked erect and bit her lip, already raw from biting. She extended a polite hand and forced a polite tone: "Mr. Carew! This is a surprise!"

But Cramer had also heard Guy's low answering "Jean!" So he told himself grimly, "Uh-huh, I guess I'm a bad guesser," and stood up.

XIII

Guy, without moving, said, "You look very bad. You've been here all night. You look awful."

"I . . do I?" With a swift fluttering hand Jean brushed at her hair. She tried to laugh: "I didn't know there was company, or I'd have tried to fix up."

Guy whirled fiercely on the inspector: "This is a damned outrage! It's brutal! We'll see if you can—"

"Please!" Jean was after him, catching his arm. She got in

front of him and compelled his eye. "There must—I guess you misunderstand. This has nothing to do with you, Mr. Carew, really. They are just asking me some questions about a piece of yarn which I don't care to answer. It's perfectly all right for them to ask, only I happen to be stubborn about it." She waved a hand and tried another laugh. "Let them go ahead, I don't mind. I had a good sleep and a good breakfast, and I can stand it if they can." Her voice sharpened. "You are not to interfere. It's none of your business."

Guy, frowning down at her, met her gaze and saw the significant gleam in her eye. Silence. Finally he muttered, "Your eyes are bloodshot. There's dirt on the side of your face." He moved abruptly and pushed at a chair. "Here, sit down."

"Thanks, I've been sitting all night—I mean I can stand all right." But she sat.

So did Guy. He pulled another chair within a yard of hers and, seated, gazed at her again. Finally he leveled his eyes at Cramer. "I'm much obliged to you, Inspector, for letting me see Miss Farris. I'm thinking over what she said. I'm not very quick-witted. I'm not thick, but I'm a little slow. I started to blow up a minute ago, and of course that was dumb. What you're doing with Miss Farris is either legal or it isn't. If it is, I can't stop you, and if it isn't, you'll soon be stopped by the law. But since you were good enough to let me see her, maybe you'd tell me something. I've only read the newspaper. What is she here for?"

Cramer, who had been impartially dividing his gaze between them, now let Guy have it all. "Certainly, Mr. Carew. She's here because she has vital information connected with the murder of your father and refuses to divulge it."

"What information?"

"She had in her possession some bayeta yarn identical with the piece found in your father's hand. She won't say where she got it."

"What makes you think it's identical?"

"We know it is. We got a sample from her file and compared it microscopically."

"What . . ." Guy hesitated. He went on, "What happens if she refuses to tell? I've asked a lawyer. I'm asking you."

"You're asking the right man." Cramer smiled grimly. "We'll continue to try to persuade her that it's her duty to tell. We'll do our best to show her that if she doesn't tell it creates an uncomfortable situation for her as well as for us. Except when she falls asleep—" He shrugged. "We'll fight any legal steps taken to release her, and unquestionably we'll fight successfully, with what we can show the court. I may add that if developments show that she has been shielding the actual criminal, she will be subject to prosecution as an accessory."

"I see." Guy sat. He took a look at Jean, then turned back to Cramer. He took a breath. "Well, she isn't shielding the criminal. She's shielding me. I gave—"

"Guy! *Guy!*"

"No, Jean. You sit down—I gave her that yarn myself. It was part of a jacket—Jean, damn it, do you think I can let you carry this when it belongs to me?"

"Yes, I do!" She was glaring at him. "You needn't be such a frightful snob! I was enjoying it!"

"Yes, you were. Not much. I'm not a snob—or maybe I am—you remember what I told you yesterday morning about a cad—the nuances are too fine for me." Guy returned to the inspector: "So Miss Farris got the yarn from me. Was there anything else you wanted of her?"

"That was the main thing."

"Then let her go. Send her home. You've kept her up all night and she needs rest. Send her home and I'll give you whatever details you want."

"We'll send her pretty soon." Cramer spoke as if words might shatter eggshells. "We haven't abused her any." He looked at her. "I'd like to have you confirm Mr. Carew. Did you get that yarn from him?"

"No!"

Guy stared at her. Cramer demanded, "Oh, you didn't?"

Jean's eyes were defiant at the inspector. "I didn't mean no. Nor yes either. I've told you a thousand times that I will never tell you where I got that yarn, and I won't. If Mr. Carew wants to pretend that he gave it to me, he can."

Cramer observed drily, "It looks like you don't want to go home."

"Nonsense." Guy leaned; touched her arm. "Look here, Jean. You should never have been in this at all. This is my battle and I can fight it. I release you from the promise you made. I command you to confirm what I said."

"You *command* me?"

"Yes."

"Well, of all the—" Her eyes were wide at him. "You big fool! You should never have come here! I was doing all right! And now you *command* me!"

Cramer growled, "She means she don't take orders. I could have told you that."

Guy, looking a little bewildered, had hold of Jean's elbow.

He stammered, "I only meant—damn it, I told you I don't know how to get along with women! Jean, I beg you! I beg you, Jean! I've told him anyhow. Don't be stubborn. I would never be stubborn with you."

"All right," she said shortly. "But I won't go home, not right now."

"You won't need to," Cramer assured her. "There will be a few little details. Did Mr. Carew give you that yarn?"

"Yes."

"Was it part of a jacket?"

"Yes."

"Okay— Now, Mr. Carew, the jacket. Tell me about it."

"There's not much to tell." Guy looked straight at him. "It was mine. It was made for me last April by a Choctaw woman in Oklahoma, from a piece of a bayeta blanket. I had it with me when I came East a month ago, the day before my father was killed. I showed it to two men, along with other things I had brought. That afternoon I took it with me when I went to the tennis court with Miss Tritt. I put it on after the game and wore it to the house, and left it in a closet in the side hall when I put the balls and rackets away. I told Miss Farris yesterday I wasn't positive about that, but since then I've thought about it, and now I'm sure I did, because when Buysse came I took him there and showed it to him. That was the last I saw of it for two weeks. I never thought of it or looked for it, since my mind was occupied with something else. My father had been murdered. I didn't know until four days ago that a piece of bayeta yarn had been clutched in his hand."

Guy's jaw worked. He controlled it and went on, "On Wednesday, July 21st, I met Miss Farris. A friend of mine who knew that one of my methods of trying to promote the welfare of the Indian tribes was to have them instructed in modern weaving took me to her workshop. I was extremely impressed . . . by her talents and achievements . . ." He turned his head and blurted abruptly at Jean, "Other ways too." To the inspector again: "I invited her to drive with my friend and me to Lucky Hills the following day and see some Indian things there. She came. That was Thursday the 22nd. We went into my room, and there, lying on a chair, was the jacket. As I said, I hadn't seen it since July 6th. I thought it would be—that is, I thought I would like to see Miss Farris wear something of her own design with bayeta yarn in it—the yarn that was used by the Indians centuries ago. I offered it to her and she was kind enough to take it and say she would use it. When she left, after dinner that evening, she took it along."

Guy looked at Jean. "If I had had any idea—if I could have known it would mean getting her into this—"

Jean muttered, "Forget it."

Cramer said, "Yeah. Of course at that time you didn't know the yarn had been found in your father's hand."

"No. The police saw fit to keep that secret."

Jean offered, "And of course that proves that the fact that the jacket belonged to Mr. Carew—I mean, since he didn't know the yarn had been found in his father's hand—"

Cramer grunted. "Neither did the murderer know it. If he had known it was there he would never have left it there. Not even the murderer had any reason to suppose we were interested in bayeta yarn until four days ago, when that newspaper reporter got hold of it and made the rounds. . . . Who were the two men you showed the jacket to?"

"Amory Buysse and Wilson. The Cherokee Indian."

"Yeah, I know him. When and where?"

"To Wilson, in my room, unpacking my trunks, early in the afternoon. To Buysse, in the hall closet where I had put it, around half past six."

"Did anyone else see it?"

"Yes. Miss Tritt of course, but I don't believe anything was said about it. Leo Kranz must have seen it, but I don't know whether he especially noticed it. I had it on, I suppose, when the Barths arrived and I was introduced to them. That was when we left the tennis court."

"You hung it on a hook in the closet?"

"No, on a hanger. On the rod."

"And you never thought of it again for over two weeks?"

"No. As I said, under the circumstances—"

"I know. But you were at Lucky Hills most of the time, and you wore clothes. Did you never go near that closet?"

"No. Or maybe I did. It wasn't my personal closet. Outdoor things were kept there—sweaters and so on. If I did go near it I didn't notice the jacket or think to look for it."

"In spite of the fact that it was made from an old bayeta blanket?" Cramer was slightly brusque. "As rare and valuable as that? And a gift, a keepsake? And your mind was so occupied that you never thought of it once?"

"You seem to be arguing." Guy's eyes had narrowed a little. "I'm not defending my thoughts; I'm just telling you."

"And I'm commenting on the laws of probability. You shouldn't be squeamish, sir; after all, the presumption is that your interest in this case is identical with ours. Who was the friend who went to Lucky Hills with you and Miss Farris on July 22nd?"

"Walter Vaughn of the Bureau of Indian Affairs. He had come to New York to see me."

Cramer scribbled on a pad. "In Washington now?"

"I suppose so. His office is there."

"Was he present when you found the jacket in your room and gave it to Miss Farris?"

"Yes."

"Was the jacket in good repair?"

"Not very. It was made from a piece of old damaged blanket which had never been restored. It had been cleaned, but there were a couple of small holes in it, and it was somewhat frayed."

"So that if a man had grabbed at it he might easily have pulled off a piece of yarn."

"Yes. Quite easily."

"If I put all this in the form of a statement, I suppose you'll have no objection to signing it?"

"None at all."

Jean interposed, "Wait a minute, Guy. I don't think you ought to sign anything until your lawyer sees it. Haven't you got a lawyer?"

"I had one. Sam Orlik."

"Then I think you should send for him, and you shouldn't do any more talking until he's here. I'm sure you shouldn't sign anything—"

Cramer put in smoothly, "Now, Miss Farris. Please. I submit that Mr. Carew owes us a little co-operation. After all, he had known for four days that we were moving heaven and earth in the effort to trace that yarn, and he knew all about it, and said nothing. I don't say that's suspicious, I only say—"

"But you think it's suspicious." Jean was sharp. "It was you who told me that in a murder case it's an entirely new set of rules. I understand that one of them is that you suspect everybody, and I think you have a nerve to ask for co-operation from a man under suspicion. Mr. Carew only came here because he thought I was in a hole, and I—I think it was wonderful of him to do it—"

"Certainly it was. I agree absolutely. I also agree that he should stand on his legal rights, and particularly that he should refuse to sign anything, if there was a chance that he might incriminate himself. But there isn't. You said we suspect everybody, but we can't very well suspect Carew of murdering his father when he has an airtight alibi."

"Oh! He has—"

"An alibi. Sure. He's had it from the beginning. That's another of the items the police have seen fit to keep to themselves, but I might as well relieve your mind of any fear of a murder charge against Mr. Carew. His father was killed between ten minutes to six and a quarter past seven in the morning. When Wilson, the Indian, went to the house at half past seven to report what he had discovered in the tomb, he found Portia Tritt in Guy Carew's room. An hour later she told the police that she had been there with him continuously for over five hours, since 2:00 A.M. Mr. Carew confirmed it."

Cramer saw Guy's brows meeting and his face darkening. He saw Jean's glare of incredulity, the quick intake of her gasp, and the stiffening of her body. He went on smoothly, "Since then, both of them have on various occasions repeated the statement. They both refuse to tell the object of her visit to his room, or what was being discussed during that five and one half hours, but that doesn't affect the alibi *as* an alibi." Cramer shrugged. "Some people might sort of raise their brows at it, his father's fiancée in his room with him all night, but he just said a while ago that the nuances are too fine for him. Anyhow, that's none of my—you wanted to say something, Miss Farris?"

Twice Jean's mouth had opened and closed again. She had glanced to her right for one bright instant and met Guy's dark inscrutable scowl, and hastily away. Now she gazed miserably at the inspector's blandness and said in a painfully flat voice, "I don't believe it."

Cramer shrugged again. "Ask him."

Jean turned her head, and all she saw was the scowl. She stood up. Her shoulders swayed a little, and she jerked them to rigidity. She spoke to Cramer: "I seem to have—misunderstood. I've been pretty stupid. If I may—may I go now? I'd like to go home—"

She turned and took two firm steps. Cramer made no move, but Guy did. One stride took him to her, and his grasp on her shoulders wasn't gentle. "Wait, Jean. This time I do command you—"

"Let go of me!"

"Oh, no. You listen." Guy turned her, by force, so that they were facing Cramer, and spoke to him: "You too. I let you go on talking because I deserved it. I'm not quick-witted, but I'm not too dumb to live. You were being slick. You guessed I'm in love with Miss Farris. I am. I've never been in love before, but I am now and I have been ever since I saw her, and I don't want anything as much as I want her good opinion. You saw that and you worked up to this, but I don't resent it because I was sick of the damn lie anyhow. Portia Tritt wasn't in my room five hours. She was there five minutes. She came to tell me that she had been to my mother's tomb and found my father lying there dead." Still gripping Jean's shoulders, he turned her, again by force, so that she was facing him, and demanded of her, "Do you believe me?"

She had to tilt her head far back to look up at him. He shook her a little and repeated, "Do you believe me?" Their eyes met, his down, hers up. She nodded. In a moment she nodded again. He released her and said gruffly, "Now you can go home. You're played out. You go home and go to bed."

"Oh, no." She tried a smile, but her lips trembled and she gave it up. "You can't command me twice the same day. I'm going to stay—"

Cramer's voice sounded crisply: "Will you sit down, please? I mean you, Mr. Carew. I think he's right, Miss Farris. You're free to go. In fact, you are to go."

Jean returned to her chair, sat down, met his eye and told him, "If I go I'll be carried."

Guy sat down too. The inspector looked from him to her, and finally grunted. "Okay. We'll see. . . . Now, Mr. Carew. I take it for granted that you realize what you're doing. You say it was a lie about Miss Tritt being in your room with you from two till seven thirty?"

"I do. She was there four or five minutes."

"What time did she arrive?"

"Around 7:25. I was up, and bathed and dressed, ready to go downstairs—"

"What time did you get out of bed?"

"I got out of bed twice. The first time was at 6:15; I had set the alarm. I got up and went to the window to see if the sun was shining. I stood there for perhaps twenty minutes, and there was a bright sun constantly, and I said an old Cherokee chant of gratitude."

"Because that meant your father wouldn't marry Miss Tritt?"

"Yes. Of course no Cherokee is a sun worshiper today, but I know the old chants. I lay on the bed again, but didn't go to sleep. At seven I got up and bathed and dressed. There was a knock on the door and I said come in and it was Portia Tritt. She was pale and trembling. She said my father was lying on the floor of the tomb, dead."

"How did she know that?"

"She had seen him. She had got up early and gone for a walk—I suppose she was as anxious about the sunshine as I was—and had looked inside the tomb enclosure, and had seen Wilson lying there unconscious, bound and gagged. Then she had seen that the tomb door was partly open, and had gone and looked in. She saw a body on the floor, and had entered and found it was my father."

"And went straight to your room?"

"No. I asked her about that later. She couldn't have, if she saw Wilson still bound and unconscious. She said she had been badly frightened and shocked, and I suppose she was. She said she left the enclosure at the far end, the north, and went round about to the north wing of the house, where she had left the door unlocked. She sat in her room thinking about it, and she decided that I had killed my father to keep him from marrying her. Then she decided to come to my room and see how I acted and have a talk with me. So she came."

"She actually told you all that?"

"Yes. Not all at once. It came out gradually. I saw a good deal of her after that morning."

"Yeah, I know you did. Does she still think you killed your father?"

"I don't know. I'm no good at telling what a woman thinks. She had been there only a few minutes when Wilson came. You know what happened then. Later a state policeman, Captain Goss, was asking us about our movements. It happened that I was present when he was questioning Miss Tritt. I was astonished when I heard her tell him that she was in my room with me from two o'clock until the time Wilson arrived, but my face doesn't show astonishment much. I was too bewildered to tell Captain Goss at that moment that she was lying. Then I considered it. I decided she had done it to conceal something important, perhaps even a knowledge of who the murderer was, and I thought it gave me a hold on her. I didn't realize that it gave her a hold on me. I knew that I as well as the others would be suspected by the police, and I figured her story would remove suspicion from me and leave me unhampered in my own efforts to learn the truth. I suppose it did work that way, but it hasn't helped me any to be unhampered; at least, I haven't accomplished anything. I've kept it to myself. I haven't even told my lawyer. Now it comes out like this."

"So it does." Cramer spoke slowly. "Is it out now? All of it?"

"It is. You asked me a while ago if I would sign a statement. I will. I'll dictate it myself, or you can—"

"No, thanks." Cramer compressed his lips and sat silently regarding him. Finally he heaved a sigh. "I'll tell you, Mr. Carew. If I'm going to charge a man with a crime, there's no law in this state that compels me to warn him not to incriminate himself. It's often done, but that's just courtesy; in most cases we don't bother. But naturally, you're in a special category. You're a millionaire, and you're going to have lawyers who can toss oak leaves through a window screen. You've already got Sam Orlik. So I'm much obliged, but I don't want any signed statements, to give Orlik an excuse to start yelling about duress. The next questions you answer will be asked by the district attorney."

He pushed a button on his desk. Jean stared at him, then at Guy, and Guy nodded at her grimly. She demanded, "But, Guy—what does he mean—he can't—"

Guy said, "All right, Jean. Don't worry. I'm glad that damned thing is out of my system. I want to say—in case I don't get another chance for a while—how grand you were to stick it out all night—just because you promised me. Of course I would have done as much for you, and more, because I love you, but you did it just because you had promised. That was pretty damn swell—"

The door had opened and Sergeant Burke was in the room. Cramer beckoned him to the desk.

"Is the commissioner in the building?"

"Yes, sir. He came a few minutes ago."

"Good. Phone him I'll be right up. Then phone the district attorney and tell him to come at once to the commissioner's office, urgent. Have you had a report from Portia Tritt's shadow this morning?"

"Yes, sir. She hadn't left home at ten o'clock."

"Okay. Send a man to bring her down here immediately. Better send Stebbins. I hope he gets her before she's off on a weekend—anyhow, get her no matter where she is. Leave a man in here with Miss Farris and see that she does no phoning. As soon as Portia Tritt arrives, turn Miss Farris loose and put her in a taxi. Keep Mr. Carew—"

Jean burst out, "I don't want a taxi! I'm going to stay—"

"Don't be foolish, Miss Farris. You're going home—at least, you're going out of this building— Keep Mr. Carew in McConnell's room, with two men. Search him, if he doesn't object. If he objects, watch him. He can make one phone call, to his lawyer, Sam Orlik. Nothing else. If Orlik

106

shows up—or rather when he shows up—don't let him see Mr. Carew until you get word from me or the commissioner or the district attorney. You'd better get Mr. Carew out of here first— All right, Mr. Carew?"

Guy stood up. Jean stood too, and went close to him, faced him. Her voice was steady: "Guy . . . is this the way it goes? Is there nothing to do? Simply nothing?"

He shook his head. "Thanks, Jean. Not a damn thing. It'll come—it'll work out."

"I know it will." She put out her hand. "Shake."

Cramer demanded gruffly, "Well, Burke?"

XIV

At half past eleven Eileen Delaney, haggard as to countenance and lamentably untidy as to apparel, was sitting at her desk in her office, talking on the telephone in a harsh but energetic voice.

"What do you mean, argument on the motion at two o'clock? Argument with who, the judge? Then what? When does he decide? Tomorrow or next day! That's impossible! I'm telling you, Mr. Raleigh—for God's sake, let me alone! That wasn't for you, someone's here pulling at me. I'm telling you, if she has to wait until tomorrow or next day, my opinion of justice and everything connected with it, including lawyers—wait a minute, hold the wire, I'm having my clothes pulled off—"

The tugging at her sleeve, by the chunky woman from the anteroom, did indeed seem purposeful. Miss Delaney turned to glare at her: "Can't you wait till I'm through?"

Cora said, "Miss Farris is back! She's here!"

"What? She's what?"

"She's here! She just came back! She's—"

Miss Delaney dropped the telephone, leaped from her chair, almost trampled Cora, and rushed from the room. Through another room, another door, into Jean's chamber. Jean was there at the big table, perched on her stool, her head down, buried in her crossed forearms. Miss Delaney stopped short ten feet away and made a noise in her throat.

Jean raised her head. "Oh. Hello, Eileen. I'm late to work again."

"Well, hello." Miss Delaney snorted. "You look like flotsam and jetsam. What in the name of God—"

"Please." Jean put up a hand. "Don't ask me any questions of any kind whatever. I never want to hear another question as long as I live. But I want to ask you one—right now, and get it over with. When a detective came here yesterday and asked you for a piece of yarn and you got it out of my file—"

"It wasn't a detective! It was a newspaper—"

"No. It was a detective. Investigating the Carew murder. That piece of yarn you kindly gave him has put Guy Carew in jail. Did they come for the rest of it this morning, and the scraps? I was too tired to look—anyhow, it doesn't matter now. The place doesn't seem to be messed up much."

"Yes, they came. They got it." Miss Delaney stood regarding, in mingled concern and disapproval, her partner's pallid face. "I didn't understand it, from the newspaper, and I don't understand it now. So that man was a detective. He said his name was Parker and he wanted it for publicity in the *Town and Country Register*. The clever, dirty, double-crossing, slimy crocodile."

"All right. You couldn't help it." Jean wearily brushed back her hair. "They didn't search here this morning, did they? Did they go through my desk?"

"No. They were here when I came, and they had a warrant, so I gave them the scraps and the rest of the yarn." Miss Delaney moved to the table. "Look here, Jean. If I'm responsible for all this, I'm perfectly willing to crawl off and die. I feel like a worm. What's Guy Carew in jail for? Murder?"

Jean nodded.

"Well. Can I do anything?"

"Nothing. Thanks, Eileen. Except you'll need a lot of patience. I'm afraid I won't be much good around here for a while."

Miss Delaney snorted. "Nor anywhere else. At least not today. Look at you! You ought to be in bed. Listen . . . Jean? Under the circumstances . . . I withdraw the remarks I made day before yesterday about Guy Carew. I've never seen him, and it would suit me all right if he went to Alaska and lived in a tent . . . but I'm for you twenty-four hours a day. So if there is anything I can do . . ."

"No, thanks. If there is, I'll let you know. You might tell Cora I don't want any phone calls and I don't want to see anybody."

"I will." Miss Delaney turned abruptly and left the room.

Jean let her head fall onto her arms again. Her head was no good; it was like a choked shuttle; it wouldn't work. What she ought to do was go to bed and sleep for twelve hours, but she wouldn't. It was an inexpressible relief to rest her head on her arms like this. What was it he had said just as that policeman came in the room? "Of course I would have done as much for you, and more, because I love you . . ." Surely that was direct enough. It would be impossible to say it more directly and positively than that. Then what he had said to the inspector: "You guessed I'm in love with Miss Farris. I am." That was direct too, but it was more like a cold statement of any fact, just any kind of a fact. The other was better . . . it was more . . . it was better . . . "Of course I would have done as much for you, and more, because I love you . . . because I love you . . . because I love you . . ."

She jerked her head up, jerked herself erect, blinking. So! That was how far gone she was! Putting herself to sleep by letting those words sound in her ears, inside her head, over and over again! That would be a big help, wouldn't it? But there was something she had wanted to do that might be a help—what the dickens was it—of course! She climbed down from the stool, went to the bowl in the corner alcove, and with a washcloth gave her face and neck a good dousing in cold water. After a vigorous rub she went to her desk and took some papers from the center drawer. Thank goodness Eileen hadn't made them search for the yarn and scraps! She sat down, unfolded the papers, and read the one on top:

"Thursday, August 5, 1937.
"A little after eight I went to the house, took the evening paper to my room, and spent fifteen minutes or so reading it. About 8:30 I took a shower and dressed for dinner. About 9:05 I joined the party on the terrace.
"MELVILLE BARTH."

It was written in pencil, in neat tight characters, and was reasonably legible. She reread it, frowned at it awhile, and went on to the next.

"I was withe mi frend Buyys all that time. He was and I was under a tree redy to stay to eat. And mi frend Buys sed to me now it is 9 ocloc mi frend wilson and we will see what this Mrs. barthe will have to eat for us then we come here.
"WOODROW WILSON."

That one was in letters half an inch high, crooked and sprawling. Jean thumbed through the others and pulled one from the middle:

> "I spoke a few words with Miss Farris, on the lawn where the party had been, at about ten minutes past eight. A little later, about 8:30, on the side of the house where we are now eating, Miss Tritt and three other ladies came up and we talked. About ten minutes after that, we were joined by others and I was introduced to them. The conversation was continued until we were called to the table.
>
> "GUY CAREW"

Jean put that one off to the right, by itself, and found the one signed by Portia Tritt. It agreed with Guy's. Next she read Buysse's, and found that it corroborated Wilson's. There was one, surprisingly, from Mrs. Barth; it recounted trips from guests to kitchen to butler to terrace, which obviously left no opportunity for crowding in assault and robbery at a distant spot in the grounds. She took up the last one:

> "It was about a quarter past eight when I was saying good-bye to Mrs. Davison Little and Dan Bryant, who were leaving in Bryant's car. I strolled around with a vague idea of finding Mme. Bernetta, and saw the deer in their enclosure and went to look at them. There was a group of four or five people near the fence some distance away. At one minute before nine, by my watch, I left and came to the house and was directed to this terrace.
>
> "LEO KRANZ."

Jean frowned at that one, and read it over before placing it with the others. As near as she could see, the papers were very little help. She hadn't needed evidence to prove that Guy Carew had not knocked her on the head. As for the others, either Kranz or Barth might be suspected, and of course it was quite possible that although Buysse and Wilson had been together, they had not been sitting under a tree. And the cold water on her face and neck hadn't helped her head any; she simply didn't have the energy to hold it up and think both at the same time; but she must think;

110

her arms were folded on the desk and her head went down to them. . . .

Something had hold of her shoulder, and a voice was irritatingly and persistently repeating her name.

"Jean! Jean! Jean, wake up!"

She struggled, and was erect. "What— Oh, Eileen. What —good lord! I went—what time is it?"

"One o'clock. Ten after. There's a man here—I tried to chase him, and couldn't. His name is Orlik. Guy Carew's lawyer."

"Orlik?" Jean got to her feet. She brushed at her hair. "Orlik. Yes, that's right." She blinked and rubbed her eyes. "I want to see him. Send him in here."

"You've had no lunch. You ought to be—"

"Ask Cora to bring me a sandwich and coffee. Two or three sandwiches. I realize I'm starving."

After a few more protestations, which Jean waved aside, Eileen went. The door opened to admit Sam Orlik. He introduced himself, waited for Jean to offer a hand, took it with the proper flavor of formality, and accepted an invitation to a chair. The aim of his pale eyes at her face could not have been called a stare, but it made Jean uncomfortable. She had been stared at all night, with that maddening light blazing in her eyes. . . .

He said conversationally, "I have a message for you from my client, Mr. Guy Carew. He wishes to apologize for the trouble he has caused you. I told him it would be necessary for me to see you as soon as possible, and he wishes to apologize for that also."

"That's silly," Jean declared. "Is he—did they keep him—"

"He's under arrest, yes. For murder. He is now on his way to White Plains—the crime was in Westchester County."

"That's silly too. How can they arrest a man for murder when it's obvious he didn't do it?"

"Well, obvious—" Orlik shrugged. "I was a little surprised myself that they shot the murder charge, but of course their tongues have been hanging out for a month and their nerves are upset. I don't know if I would say they're silly. Mr. Carew had motive—aside from his father's intended marriage and other complications, an heir to a great fortune always has motive, naturally. He had opportunity. The fact that the yarn came from a jacket which he owned is a damaging bit of circumstantial evidence. Very damaging. Worst of all— it would be for a jury—is his offering a false alibi."

"He didn't offer it! Portia Tritt—"

"He accepted it, he confirmed it, and later he repeated it." Orlik shrugged, and added drily, "Now he admits he lied. That's very bad. I may be able to keep it away from the jury; I certainly intend to try."

"That's twice you've mentioned a jury." Jean was frowning. "Surely—do you mean there's a chance that there will actually be a trial? In a courtroom?"

"They hold them in courtrooms. Whether they can convict or not—they certainly have enough to make it a hard case."

"My God." Jean stared. "I hadn't supposed—I supposed their arresting him only meant he would have to explain—they couldn't possibly *convict* him—"

"You're quite an optimist. So is Mr. Carew." Orlik sighed. "I'll tell you, Miss Farris, I'm going to be pretty frank with you, and in case you wonder why I'll tell you. I figure that after your performance last night, holding out against Cramer and Skinner, you can be trusted, and God knows Carew needs someone he can trust. I'd like to ask you, when they kept after you for fourteen hours to tell them where you got that yarn, why didn't you tell?"

"Because I had promised I wouldn't."

"Promised Mr. Carew?"

"Yes."

"Then are you a good friend of his? A real friend? Right on through?"

"I don't know what you mean by 'right on through.' I'm a good and real friend of Guy Carew."

"Enough so you'd go to some trouble to keep him from being tried and convicted and electrocuted for murdering his father?"

"Of course—" Jean shivered, then her shoulders were held rigid. "That's incredible. It's monstrous. But of course I would."

"Good. That's fine. As I said, I think you can be trusted. I hope to God you can. Don't think I'm rushing you unnecessarily, because I'm not. I'm being frank with you. Cramer was a fool to let you go, and Skinner and Anderson are a pair of nincompoops not to nab you right now and get you under heavy bond. They're apt to realize that any minute, and that's why there's no time to lose. Here's what I want you to do. The *Rosaria* sails in less than five hours, at six o'clock. You go down there now, and I mean now, and get on board. I considered details in the taxi coming up here. Your name will be Ruth Gunther. There'll be a man there within an hour with a couple of thousand cash for you, and a ticket—now wait a minute, wait till I—"

"Nonsense! You mean run away? Me? Why should I?"

"Because you're the key witness in the case against Guy Carew. Because if you don't—"

He stopped abruptly at a knock on the door and the sound of the knob turning, and turned his head sharply. But it was only Eileen Delaney, with a tray holding three sandwiches, two éclairs, and a container of coffee. Jean tried to wave it away, but Miss Delaney paid no attention. She placed the tray before her partner, removed the lid of the container, made a curt remark about the foolishness of starving, and departed. Sam Orlik gazed at the door after it had closed behind her, listening to the retreating footsteps from the other side, and then turned to Jean:

"That your lunch? Go ahead, don't mind me. Get it down. I was saying, you're going to be the key witness for the state. Their most damaging piece of evidence, by far, will be the fact that the yarn found in Val Carew's hand came from his son's jacket. But they can't possibly prove it without you. They can't produce the jacket, because it doesn't exist any more. Any piece of yarn or scrap of material they try to introduce, I can absolutely have it excluded, because they can't show it came from Guy's jacket. I understand you unraveled the jacket with your own hands, and you did the weaving yourself. That right?"

Jean nodded.

Orlik nodded back. "There you are. They'll fuss around with it, but if I can't keep it out I'd better start chasing ambulances. Without you on the witness stand, the yarn simply can't get into the case at all. And with the yarn out, I'll stand a better than even chance of licking them. After it's over you can come back. Of course all your expenses will be paid, and they don't need to be modest expenses, since there's plenty of money—now, what are you shaking your head for? Didn't you say you're a good friend of Guy Carew?"

"I am."

"Well, haven't I made it plain enough?"

"You've made it perfectly plain." Jean's gaze was level at him. "Several things. But maybe I'm wrong. You sound as if you believe Guy—Mr. Carew is guilty. And he isn't."

Orlik gestured impatiently. "That's immaterial. We won't get anywhere discussing that, though I might mention that he deceived me, his attorney, about that Portia Tritt alibi. But that has nothing to do with it. My job is to get him turned loose if I can, and if he is tried, get him acquitted. That's all I'm interested in, and that's all I want, and under the cir-

113

cumstances, believe me, that's all anyone has a right to expect. And if you are his friend, and if you are intelligent enough to take the judgment of a man who has been through—"

"No!" Jean was emphatic. "You mean run away. I won't do that. I don't even ask you if Guy knew you were going to ask me to, because I know he didn't. Did he?"

"No. It's our job, his friends' job—"

"I knew he didn't. He wouldn't want me to run away. And if you, his lawyer, if you think he's guilty, I think that's shameful. I not only know he is innocent, I have proof of it. Written proof."

Orlik's eyes widened. "You have what? Written by whom?"

"I have proof. Wait." Jean clambered from the stool, went to her desk for the papers she had left there, and returned with them and handed them to him. "There. Read those."

The lawyer took them, got nose glasses from his pocket, and went through them, rapidly but methodically. He removed the glasses, holding them in his fingers, and demanded, "Well?"

"Well, that proves Guy is innocent." Jean was back on the stool. "Did you know that on Thursday evening someone knocked me on the head and stole my skirt and jacket?"

"Yes. Carew told me about it yesterday, when he gave me the sample of yarn you gave him. I presume these are the reports of their activities made by the guests at Mrs. Barth's request."

"They are. Do you notice what Guy wrote? Do you notice that from half past eight till nine o'clock he was with several people and it can be confirmed by them? Don't you realize that the murderer had got in a panic because he had learned of the yarn found in Val Carew's hand, and he knew the yarn in my suit must be the same and could be traced, and so he followed me, or found me, and took it?"

"And so?" Orlik asked calmly.

"So it couldn't have been Guy Carew!" Jean was shrill. "Good Lord, don't you see? If it was the murderer who took my suit, and if Guy was somewhere else when that happened—"

"Sure, I see." Orlik thrust the papers into his pocket and sat back. "I'm going to ask you to let me take these; there might possibly be a use for them, though I doubt it. Your deductions from them are full of holes. Your hypothesis that it was the murderer himself who assaulted and robbed you is pure assumption; it might have been done for another reason, or it might have been done by a confederate—

Buysse or Wilson or both of them, or even Kranz or Barth—and it has no effect on the evidence regarding the murder itself. And it's so far from proving Carew innocent that it would even add to the presumption of his guilt. Who else knew that the yarn in your suit had come from his jacket? If he was the only one who knew that—"

"He wasn't. They all knew it. Someone asked me where I got the yarn—it was Portia Tritt—and I told them. They were all there together."

The lawyer shrugged. "Even so, it doesn't prove anything. Another point: I suppose you have a good memory, and if you go on the stand you will probably remember that Carew went to you and asked you to promise to say nothing about the jacket he had given you. Imagine a jury chewing on that. That will be just fine."

"Well . . . I don't know. I . . . I might not remember it . . . if I had to. . . . Oh, I hope it won't come to that! Surely there is a way. . . ."

"You *hope!*" Orlik jumped up and leaned at her; his voice was low compressed scorn. "You and your miserable feeble little hope! And you say you're his friend! One hell of a friend you are Miss Farris! One *hell* of a friend!" His pale eyes gleamed to annihilate her; she didn't know that she was witnessing a sample of the famous spontaneous combustion of Sam Orlik, usually reserved for the courtroom. "No, I didn't tell Guy Carew I was going to ask you to run away—thank God I didn't! Thank God he'll never know that you're too brave and fine to run away! He won't even know it when he's sitting in the electric chair waiting for them to turn the juice on; he won't know, unless I explain it to him, that of all the people who helped to put him there, you"—he pointed a rigid finger—"are the bravest and the finest! Friend! Good God!"

"That—" Jean stopped because she didn't want her voice to tremble. She tried to control it: "That won't help any. That's just silly heroics."

Orlik had turned his back; he whirled again. "Oh, you sneer at heroics? You sneer, do you?" He lifted his hands and dropped them; the gleam faded from his eyes. "Let me tell you something, Miss Farris." His voice was calm and persuasive. "I've seen this happen time and time again. It's always with optimists like you. You won't pay the price because you think you won't have to. Then the day comes when panic hits you and you'd be willing to pay twice over, a hundred times, but you can't, because you're insolvent. In this case I hope to heaven that day never comes . . . but I always hope that, and sometimes it comes anyway. Now let's discuss this thing like reasonable people. . . ."

An hour later Sam Orlik departed, defeated. In the end he had tried to compromise on something more temporary and less ambitious, a mere excursion to another state; but Jean resisted even that. She wouldn't run away.

At half past two she was still perched on her stool, chewing mechanically and methodically on the sandwiches and drinking lukewarm coffee from the container. Now and then a little shiver ran over her. The food had no taste at all, and it was an effort to swallow. A little thought flitted like a momentary shadow among all the others which were chasing around in her head: that she would probably have indigestion, and that too would be a new experience. She frowned it out of the way, and went on chewing and trying to think.

There must be some way, there simply must be, of learning the truth. Could facts actually be buried so that no one could ever find them? And, not finding them, could people actually go ahead and do something so horrible, so unspeakable . . . but that wouldn't do. That was hysterical drivel, and wouldn't help any. Certainly facts could get buried and certainly people could do horrible things. The point was to prevent it. She must really *think*.

Mechanically she reached for the last sandwich. . . .

At three o'clock, with an air of decision, she pulled the telephone to her, put it to her ear and dialed a number. There was a wait of a few moments, then she made an inquiry and a request, and after that a long wait followed. Finally she spoke again:

"Mrs. Barth? I hope I didn't interrupt anything important. This is Jean Farris. It's much better, thank you, it still aches a little, nothing to speak of. Yes, I suppose you did. Yes, it is dreadful, in the papers like that, but there it is and I don't suppose it will kill me. I want to ask you a favor, a very great favor. Of course you haven't heard that Guy Carew is under arrest. . . . Oh, of course, the radio. Yes. Yes. I'm sure you didn't, neither did I. What I want to ask you is to arrange to have Mr. Barth, Mr. Kranz, Mr. Buysse, and Mr. Wilson—the Indian—at your house this evening at half past eight o'clock. I realize that perfectly, I said it is a very great favor, and you must know I wouldn't ask it if it weren't of vital importance. I know that, Mrs. Barth, and I assure you I wouldn't make such a peculiar request. . . . Yes, it is connected with the arrest, in a way. No, certainly not. No, just those four, it won't be necessary to include Miss Tritt. The newspapers and the police know nothing about it, and they won't know, I give you my word. It will be a great favor to me, and I hope and believe it will also be one to Guy Carew. Yes, it will have to be at half past eight, and they must all be there or it won't do any good. No, thank you very much. . . ."

She hung up, sat a moment frowning, looked in the book for a number, and dialed again.

She made three more telephone calls in succession. The first was to the office of a theatrical agent on Broadway, and since it was a Saturday afternoon in August, the fact that repeated attempts got no answer was not surprising and therefore no great disappointment. The second was to the editorial office of *Variety*, where she talked for three minutes with a hoarse and hearty man whose name she didn't learn, and who gave her so obvious a suggestion that she was ashamed not to have thought of it herself. The third was the headquarters of the Federal Broadcasting Company, and there, after some difficulty, she got through to the man she wanted.

"Mr. Marley? . . . Of course you didn't recognize the name Jean Farris. . . . Oh. Thank you for being delicate about it; I forgot the morning papers had made me famous. I met you a couple of months ago at Allen Lockhart's penthouse, but of course you've forgotten. I had on a yellow dress and I stepped on you when we danced, and you invited me to come to the FBC studios and be personally escorted by you, but of course that doesn't distinguish me. Anyway, you did invite me, and now I'm in trouble and need some help. . . . No, nothing like that, what I want is a man who can imitate birds. . . . No, birds, birds that sing. I know you have people who imitate all sorts of sounds, and I want a man who can imitate a whippoorwill, and I must have him by seven o'clock. . . . Of course not, I didn't suppose you would have him right there, but surely you know where you can get hold of one. No, I must have him by seven o'clock today or it won't do any good. You are wonderful and I promise never to step on you again. You can call me here, my number is— no. If you don't mind, I'd rather come to your place and wait, that would save a little time. I'll have to listen to him and see if he's good enough. I'll be there inside of half an hour. . . ."

XV

At one o'clock Inspector Cramer had offered Portia Tritt to District Attorney Anderson of Westchester County, but Anderson had begged him to keep her and carry on; and had accompanied the request with such glowing praise of the energy and brilliance which Cramer had already displayed that it would have been churlish not to acquiesce. So orders had been issued to serve a tray lunch to Miss Tritt in the private room she was being permitted to monopolize, while Cramer had eaten with the commissioner. Afterwards over an hour was consumed by the urgencies of a misunderstanding among racketeers in the Fillmore Market district and a suspicious suicide on West End Avenue; and it was after three o'clock when the inspector was again alone in his office and was able to tell Sergeant Burke to bring Miss Tritt.

Burke said, "She's got holes gnawed in the door."

Cramer nodded wearily. "Sure. Pull her out through one of them."

He arose when Burke escorted her in, waited till she was seated, and then resumed his chair and screwed up his lips at her. She certainly knew how to dress, he thought, and she also knew how to carry it, he would hand that to her. And though her gray eyes looked indignant and scrappy, there was also a wary caution in them. Quite a woman. And a godawful liar.

She was saying, "I've been kept here over four hours. I know it's useless to start screaming, but I came without protest when you sent for me, and it's outrageous and unreasonable to isolate me like a criminal and keep me waiting four hours."

Cramer said, "Uh-huh. I know it is. I'm sorry. I apologize. So now let's make it as brief as we can. A few little things have come up since I saw you yesterday afternoon. For instance, you were telling me that at 11:25, that night at Lucky Hills, you went outdoors to see what the weather looked like, and because it was cool you went first to the side hall to get a jacket."

He opened a drawer of his desk, took out a folded paper, opened it up, and walked over to her. "Here. This is a diagram of the ground floor of the house. Would you show me which hall and which closet it was that you got the jacket?"

She took the paper and studied it a moment, then pointed with a finger. "That one." He stooped to look, then retrieved the paper, folded it, and returned to his chair.

"Much obliged. I believe that's the closet where the tennis balls and rackets are kept?"

"Yes."

"Was it your own jacket you got?"

"No, nothing of mine was there. I didn't want to go upstairs. A lot of miscellaneous stuff was in that closet."

"What kind of jacket was it you took?"

"I don't know." She hesitated. "I really don't remember."

"When you came back in, at one o'clock, did you return it to that closet?"

"No. It was out of my way, going to my room, so I wore it . . . no, I didn't either. I remember that. I was in the upper hall before I remembered I had it on and it wasn't mine, so I took it off and left it there in the hall, on the arm of a seat under a mirror."

"That was in the north wing?"

"Yes, my room was in the north wing."

"Was the jacket still there in the morning?"

"I don't know. I didn't notice, and it was so dark—" She caught herself abruptly and her eyes flickered, then she went on with admirable calm, "I mean, in all the excitement, when I left Guy Carew's room—"

"That's all right," Cramer put in. "Don't mind a little slip like that. We'll discuss that in a minute, but right now let's finish with the jacket. Maybe you remember that Guy had a jacket with him at the tennis court that afternoon, and when you finished he put it on and wore it back to the house."

She nodded. "Yes."

"Did you notice that jacket particularly?"

"Not—I wouldn't say particularly. I saw it was an old Indian weave—an antique—it had holes in it."

"Did you know the red yarn in it was called bayeta? Did he tell you about it?"

"Not that I remember."

Cramer grunted. "Okay. That jacket—the one that Guy wore—was left by him in that side hall closet—the one you showed me on the diagram—when he put the balls and rackets away. Was it that one that you took at 11:25 that night to wear outdoors?"

"I've told you, I don't remember what kind of jacket I took."

"Do you remember that it was not that jacket?"

"No."

"It—" She stopped, then at once went on, "It could have been, yes."

"And whatever jacket you took, you left it in the upper hall of the north wing and you don't know whether it was there in the morning or not?"

"That's what I told you, Inspector."

"And that's the truth?"

"Really—" Her eyes flickered. Then she lifted a hand and dropped it, and shrugged her shapely shoulders. "Yes, that's the truth."

Cramer leaned back and regarded her in silence. At length he sighed and started again, "You know, Miss Tritt, there are two or three ways of doing what I'm going to do now. I could easily ask you some trick questions that would put sweat on your brow, excuse the expression. That might be fun and it would serve you right, but it would be a waste of time. The quickest and best way is just to tell you that we know you've lied from the beginning about what you did that night between 2:00 A.M. and 7:25. The last time you did it was yesterday afternoon, to me. Well, that's out. That lie's no good any more. So suppose you go ahead and tell me what you really did do."

Portia Tritt was smiling at him, but the smile was confined to her lips, for her eyes were too intent on their specific job to join in. She said with a little laugh, "Really, Inspector! Of all the tricks, why do you pick that one? It's the most obvious of all."

"It's not a trick this time." Cramer sounded patient. "I'm telling you straight. Of course you're stubborn and you're intelligent, and you'll take some persuading. I expected that. I suppose if I told you that Guy Carew has been arrested under a charge of murder, and gave you my word of honor on it, you wouldn't believe that either."

She smiled again. "Certainly not. Would you expect me to believe that sort of nonsense?"

With a grunt Cramer pushed a button on his desk. He observed grimly, "If it wasn't for the waste of time, I swear to God I'd lock you up till this time tomorrow and see what you think of it then. Did you ever hear of something called obstructing justice? And something nicer still, conspiring to obstruct justice?—Oh, Burke, are the rags out with it yet?"

"Yes, sir. All of 'em."

"Got one?"

"Yes, sir."

"Bring it here."

He sat and looked at her. The smile had left her lips, and the banners of indignation and defiance no longer flew in her eyes, but they were quite steady. When Sergeant Burke re-entered she didn't turn around, and she gave him only a casual glance as he passed on his way to the desk to hand his superior a newspaper. Cramer waved it away: "Give it to Miss Tritt."

She took it and it screamed at her:

GUY CAREW ARRESTED FOR MURDER!

Then Cramer lost her face, for it was bent over the paper, bent low. It took her minutes to read what there was of it on the front page, and Cramer let her alone; but when her eyes moved up to the top again and she started over he interrupted brusquely:

"Once is enough, huh? I don't suppose you suspect me of forging a newspaper. That would be a trick. Have they got your name in it?"

She lifted her head, and the paper fell from her knees to the floor. Apparently she had forgotten to breathe while reading, for her whole body shook with the urgency of a shivering inhalation.

"My God," she muttered. "It's ghastly."

"Yeah, it usually is. I warn you, Miss Tritt, there'll be no tendency around here, or at White Plains either, to let you down easy. You did obstruct justice. You told the police a lie that gummed the works from the beginning, and you stuck to it. There's only one thing to do now, come absolutely clean, and be darned careful while you're at it. Tell me now exactly what you did do that night from two o'clock on."

Her shoulders sagged. "But it says there—" Her hand fluttered to indicate the paper on the floor. "And in the headlines. . . . Good God." She stared at the paper.

Suddenly she straightened up and looked at Cramer. "At any rate," she declared, "you can't expect me to tell you anything now. I must have a lawyer. You can't expect—"

Cramer blurted, "It's not what I expect. I'll just tell you what I'm going to do. If you come clean with me here and now so I can start a check up, I won't keep you and I won't put a charge on you. Not for the present at least, if the check up is good. If you hold me up by calling a lawyer in and trying to cover with legalities, I'll keep you on two counts, as a material witness and also under a charge of obstructing justice. You'll get out on bail, of course, but you'll have a charge to beat, and there'll be no consideration shown around here, or in the district attorney's office either. Take your pick. You can phone your lawyer right now if you want to—here's a phone."

"But if I really have obstructed justice—I ought to know—"

"That's your funeral. Take your pick."

She sat and stared at the newspaper, her lips pressed tight, her brows drawn together, stiff and motionless. After a while she muttered, "It's hard to think straight, with—under the circumstances." She sat and stared some more.

Suddenly she pulled herself up, looked Cramer in the eye, and told him, "All right. You say if I tell you what I did I can go. Everything happened as I said it did up to two o'clock. I returned to the house at one and went to my room and sat there. Around two I went to bed, and I slept some, but not much and not very soundly. At half past five I was out of bed again, and a little later I got dressed. At six thirty exactly, which was the time the rays of the sun were supposed to come through the walls of the tomb, I left the house at the end of the north wing corridor and cut right across the lawn and through the grove of evergreens. I must have—"

"See anyone?"

"No. Not a sign of anyone. I must have got to the tomb enclosure about twenty minutes to seven, or a little before. What I intended to do was to be at the gap when Val Carew came out. I stepped into the gap and saw the Indian on the ground. His hands and feet were tied with strips of his shirt, and he was gagged. Then I saw the door of the tomb was partly open, and I ran to it and tried to see through the opening, but it was only a crack, so I pushed it wider, and saw something on the floor. I went in, and it was Val Carew, and he was dead. I kneeled down by him to make sure, and then I stood up, and I don't know how long I stood there. When I left I could see the Indian lying over by the gap, but I didn't go out of the enclosure that way. I went around and left by the gap at the other end, and kept beyond the shrubbery to circle back to the house, because I didn't want anyone to see me. Perhaps that was foolish, but I only half knew what I was doing. I got back in by the door I had left unlocked and went to my room and undressed and got into bed. I had decided to let no one know I had been out. But lying there in bed—"

She shivered. "It was horrible. Val Carew lying dead out there, and no one knowing, and time going on all over that house. . . . I got up and dressed again and went to Guy's room and knocked on the door and went in. He was up and dressed. I told him. He was so stunned he couldn't believe me, and I was still telling him when there was another knock on the door. It was the Indian. He had come to and worked himself loose and gone to the tomb—"

"Yeah, I know. While you were in the tomb why did you take that lance from the wall and why did you go up the stone steps to the platform?"

"I didn't." She stared. "Oh, you mean my fingerprints. But I've told you how they got there. Val Carew took me—"

"Was that the truth maybe?"

"It was." She looked in his eyes. "I realize I'm handicapped now. I told a lie, and everything I say is suspected. But I told that one lie, and that's all."

"Maybe. You've just described how you lay in bed after you got back from the tomb, feeling horrible. Guy Carew says that you told him that you decided he had killed his father and you went to his room to see how he would act. How about it?"

"I . . . I didn't. That isn't true."

"You mean you didn't tell him that?"

"Possibly I told him something like that. Much later. But I didn't really—I was much too shocked—"

"I'll bet you were. I'd hate to tell you, Miss Tritt, what I think it would take to shock you. And I'm warning you, if you don't give me everything straight this time, you *will* be shocked. Why did you tell the police you had been in Guy's room from two o'clock on? When did you think that up?"

"I didn't think it up. It just . . . I knew, of course, that he would be suspected, and I knew he couldn't be guilty, and I thought it would save him embarrassment, even misery—"

"Isn't it true that you and Guy thought it up together? That you concocted it in his room?"

"No! We didn't!"

"Isn't it true that he admitted his guilt and you agreed to shield him—"

"No. Why should he admit guilt? He wasn't guilty."

"Isn't it true that you made a bargain with him that if he would marry you, you would provide him with an alibi to safeguard him from a charge of murder?"

That, or something like it, went on for four hours.

The end, which came a little after seven o'clock, was not

an end in the sense that it arrived at a goal; it was more like the end of a quarter in a football game, a recess to stave off mutual exhaustion. Cramer was hoarse, for something in the personality of Portia Tritt made it impossible for him to keep his voice down; and she was clenching her fists to keep herself halfway under control, for she was disarmed, at his mercy, and dared no offense. But essentially she surrendered nothing. All Cramer had on her, at the finish, was that she had lied about her movements on the fatal night, and he had had that when they began.

But he let her go. He had said he would; and besides, there was no good reason to keep her. When she got to her feet she was trembling, but soon had herself composed; and a few minutes later, down on the street, she appeared quite natural and her voice was quite steady as she gave a taxi driver the address of Nyasset House.

XVI

Melville Barth's frosty eyes glittered with annoyance. He demanded irritably of his wife, "How the devil could I? He's in jail charged with murder. Hutchings & Osborn want blood. The brokers say they're out of it, they're only bookkeepers. The final settlement must be by Tuesday noon, and I can't settle. For God's sake quit asking me about it, it only aggravates me. And this idiotic business—these people downstairs—why did you agree to it?"

"Haven't I told you?" Mrs. Barth sighed. "She said it would be a favor to Guy Carew. And after all, Mel, it was in our house, at least on our grounds, that she was beaten unconscious and had her clothes stolen and had to walk to our door and ring the bell in her underwear. If that happened to me anywhere—at Mabel Clement's place, for instance—" Mrs. Barth shivered. "Anyhow, I told her I'd do it, and they're all waiting downstairs and you're supposed to be there. Another thing, I thought if I didn't humor her there's no telling how much trouble she could make—I had enough of it with those three detectives this morning, all over the place and asking questions and poking around, climbing the fence and falling into the shrubbery—"

"Very well. It can't be helped. I'll be down shortly."

"No, now. That's why I came up again. It's a quarter to nine, and Miss Farris says she wants to be there with us at exactly the same time as it happened, which I admit seems silly, maybe the knock on the head did really affect her brain—"

"A lot of damned female nonsense," Barth growled; but he put on a coat and followed his wife downstairs.

Two minutes later a procession of six people left the house and took the circling path to the right towards the farther driveway. Jean Farris and Mrs. Barth were in the lead; behind them was Leo Kranz and then Barth; and Amory Buysse and Woodrow Wilson were in the rear. Buysse was dressed approximately as he had been on Thursday, but Wilson wore his overalls with blue shirt and red tie, and no hat. They followed the others across the graveled drive, and another broad expanse of clipped lawn, along the edge of the cutting garden with outbuildings at one end, and through a wide stretch of meadow grass. From there the boundary fence of the estate could be seen, almost completely concealed by a riot of shrubbery. The goal, apparently, was ten yards short of it, for there Jean stopped, brushing the edge of a dense thicket of birch saplings.

Mrs. Barth nodded. "This is the place, all right. See, Mel, how they trampled those clumps of violets? No, over there. They told me they found it by looking for the spot where Miss Farris had lain down—right there, they showed me when I came to look—of course it's nearly dark now and you can't see it very well—and they thought they found where he went to the wall, probably to throw the clothes over it—only they didn't find any sign on the outside, but of course it's all stones there and there wouldn't be any footprints if he did come back later to get them—is that right, Miss Farris, is this it? I suppose it is, since you brought us here."

Jean nodded. "I know it by that bush, the one with berries." Her heart was pumping. The dusk was thickening fast, and she was afraid she wouldn't be able to see well enough; and even if she could have seen better, her elaborate scheme seemed fantastic and even silly, now that the moment had come to try it. It would all depend on one swift instant, one fraction of a second, and while the theory was all right, the successful application of it by her looked hopeless. . . .

Buysse and Wilson, who had first stopped ten feet off, had moved up in the gathering twilight to take a look at the spot Mrs. Barth had indicated. Leo Kranz asked, "Which way were you lying? Where was your head?"

Melville Barth observed icily, "I believe, Miss Farris, you wanted us here for some sort of experiment?"

"Yes," Jean said. "I had some sort of an idea, when I phoned Mrs. Barth, that we might do some investigating together, but I didn't know then that detectives had been all over it. Anyway, it's getting dark. But there's one thing I'd like to try—first, I want to show all of you exactly where I was lying." She moved. "My head was right here. Come closer, Mr. Wilson, if you don't mind, I want the opinion of all of you—you too, Mr. Buysse. My head was there, and I was on my back with my eyes closed, and—I don't believe I've mentioned this before—I heard a noise—"

Everybody jumped. Not at Jean's words, but at a shrill earsplitting note that shattered the air. Jean, not of course herself startled, had her eyes strained to watch them. She had spent hours thinking about this moment, and had reached conclusions about it, but it happened so swiftly and her faculties were all so concentrated in her eyesight that she didn't immediately realize that her conclusions had been completely justified. It happened precisely as she had calculated: when that piercing note sounded, five heads had turned with a jerk and five pairs of eyes had sought to penetrate the surrounding gathering gloom; but then, almost immediately, one of the pairs of eyes, and only one, had turned swiftly to look at her and she had met them; and he stood so close to her that even through the dusk she could see the change when the eyes realized what they were doing. They turned from her again.

There was movement among the others. Mrs. Barth was exclaiming, "My God, it scared me to death! But we were talking—I never heard of a whippoorwill—good heavens, what have you got there?"

That was for Buysse, who had acted. He had dashed into the thicket of birch at their elbows, there had been the sound of a brief scramble, and now he emerged dragging something. They all stared. Jean muttered weakly, "Oh, please, please—" but no one heard her. They were staring at Buysse's catch as he dragged it closer and stood it up, grasping its collar. Leo Kranz stepped closer to take a look. Mrs. Barth cried, "But what—what—"

Barth demanded coldly, "Who the devil are you and what were you doing in there?"

The man gulped, with Buysse still gripping his collar. He was at least a foot shorter than Buysse, with a little black mustache, big ears, and his eyes popping out. He gulped again. Barth demanded, "Well?"

Jean saw there was no way out of it. She moved over beside him: "Let go of him, Mr. Buysse. It's all right, he's—he's a friend of mine. May I—Mrs. Barth, this is Mr. Tamber. Mr. Roy Tamber. I brought him with me when I came."

"You brought him—Miss Farris, this is ridiculous—"

Tamber found his voice: "I didn't expect—I didn't know—"

"All right, Mr. Tamber, I'm sorry. I'll pay you double." Jean was trembling with excitement; she couldn't help it. "I may as well explain, because it's all over anyway. I said I wanted to try an experiment, and I did. I brought Mr. Tamber with me and smuggled him in here. He makes noises for the Federal Broadcasting Company, and I wanted him to be a whippoorwill, because a whippoorwill sang close to me Thursday evening, just before someone struck me. I wanted—"

Barth put in impatiently, "Absolute insanity. I don't want people smuggled into my grounds—"

"Of course you don't, Mr. Barth. I didn't want to be knocked unconscious in your grounds, either, and I wanted to find out who did it. I assure you I'm not insane, and one proof of it is that I did find out who struck me."

"My dear child—"

"Yes, Mrs. Barth, I did. I know now, absolutely and conclusively, which one of you came from behind those bushes Thursday evening and hit me on the head and took my clothes. I can't prove it, not yet. But there must be a way to prove it, and I'll find it somehow. I want to thank you, Mrs. Barth, for giving me the chance to do this. Come on, Mr. Tamber, I'll smuggle you out again."

She moved. Tamber, who had been released, moved after her.

"But, Miss Farris, you must explain—"

"I think the rest of us have a right—"

But Jean, with Mr. Tamber trotting after her, was gone into the dusk.

As, in Jean's roadster, they rolled along the curving secondary road leading to Portchester, Mr. Tamber cleared his throat and finally found his voice. "Of course—" There was a squeak, and he cleared his throat again and started over. "Of course I knew there might be some danger involved in it. I agreed to it, really, for the adventure. I didn't mention it to you, but you must have known I had read all about you in the morning paper. Quite an unusual name, Jean Farris."

Jean, driving, muttered assent. Her mind, to put it mildly, was occupied. Mr. Tamber went on, "I've been an artist now nearly twenty years, and this is the first time my work has been directly connected with a murder. It was an adventure, all right, but I wouldn't care to repeat it. That fellow would make a good weight lifter in a circus. What did you say his name was? Miss Farris?"

"I beg your pardon?"

"That fellow that hauled me out. What's his name?"

"Buysse."

"Oh, yes. Odd name. As I say, I knew it was connected with a murder, and I like adventure, always have, but I wouldn't have agreed to do it if I hadn't needed the money. I've followed the Carew case pretty close. It was a treat to see that Indian, a real treat. Most of the folks I talk with think the Indian did it, but when I saw the paper this evening and saw they had arrested Guy Carew, I said to myself, well, they've got the right one at last, but it certainly took them long enough. . . ."

He went on talking, as they rolled into Portchester, turned right on the Post Road, and continued south. Jean was aware that now and then he turned to look behind them, but there was no interruption to his verbal flow. The lights of a thousand cars flashed by, and a thousand thoughts flashed along the avenues of her mind, but it was impossible to shut her ears completely to his voice, or even to his words. Finally, and abruptly, she told him:

"I've just remembered that I have to make a stop this side of Larchmont, to call on somebody, and I don't know how long it will take. It might be hours. Do you mind if I drop you off at the Rye railroad station? There's sure to be a train before long."

Mr. Tamber said that would suit him fine. And that reminded him that for years he had been universally conceded to be the best imitator of a train whistle in the country. . . .

They rolled into the Rye station plaza, circled a parked truck, and came to a stop. Jean offered a good-bye, together with an expression of gratitude for his performance and regret for its unfortunate sequel. But Mr. Tamber made no move to open his door; and Jean suddenly exclaimed, "Oh, my lord, I forgot, I haven't paid you! Will it be all right if I mail you a check?"

"Well . . . a check would do." He sounded doubtful. "The fact is, I could use the cash."

"Oh." Jean hastily got into her bag and explored. "I said I would pay you double, but I don't believe I have that much . . . here's thirty dollars, will that do? I'll send you a check for the balance."

"This is quite all right." Mr. Tamber took the twenty and two fives and made their edges flush and neatly folded them. "I assure you this is adequate." He flung the door open and climbed out. "Good-bye, Miss Farris, good-bye, and thank you." He had backed off a step, but now he came close again, stuck his head in the window, and said in a tone low and hurried but carefully clear, "You ought to know that that car stopped under a tree at the far end, New York TZ9205, has been following us ever since we left." Then he whirled and trotted off, and was on the station portico before Jean realized what he had said; and before she could act on the impulse to call to him, he had disappeared inside.

She stared at the station door which had closed behind him, minded to go after him. But she had had enough of Mr. Tamber for the evening, and besides, in his devotion to adventure he had probably been imagining things. She peered the length of the plaza and saw that there was a car parked under a tree with its dim lights on, but at that distance she could make out neither its license number nor its occupant. She shrugged, engaged the clutch, rolled out of the plaza, and headed back for the Post Road.

By the time she was two miles south of Rye, some five or six minutes later, she was wishing that she had done differently—at least, that on leaving the plaza she had circled close enough to make out the license number—for it appeared certain that she was indeed being followed. The southbound traffic at that hour, ten o'clock Saturday night, was thin; thrice she had slowed down to twenty-five and then suddenly accelerated to fifty, keeping watch in the mirror, and there was unquestionably a car behind which neither overtook her when she slackened nor lost much ground when she speeded up. Her feeling was not so much alarm or even curiosity as it was indignation; whoever it might be, it was a damned impertinence. The indignation got hotter in her breast; she pressed the pedal until the speedometer showed sixty, and kept it there for a mile, until the follower had had time to get into the pace, and then suddenly stepped on the brake, hugged the curb, and came to a quick stop.

She saw in the mirror that the pursuer was stopping too, fifty yards back. That was worse than impertinent, it was insolent. With the top of the roadster down, all she had to do to get a good look was twist from under the wheel and kneel on the seat, which she did. A highway light was so placed that she couldn't make out who was in the car, through the windshield, but the license plate did show TZ9205 or something very like it. With a mutter of impatience she moved, thinking to get out and walk back, but with her hand on the door lever she stopped, arrested by a sudden little chill of fear. Even on that main highway, with cars roaring by in both directions, it was quite possible, if a man was sufficiently desperate and determined. . . .

She scrambled back behind the wheel, put the gear in, and started off. In the mirror she saw that the other car started too. All right, to the devil with him. Her speedometer went to fifty. Let him play tag if he wanted to and see what good it would do him. Fifty-five. Sixty. On a curve her tires whined, and she eased up a little. She realized that she had gone to sixty not by deliberate decision, but because the little chill of fear had spread through her blood almost to the indignity of panic, and that infuriated her. What the devil was there to be afraid of? Well—even on the lighted Post Road there were short stretches flanked by woods—and even where the lights were bright, after all, she was in an open car —and a shot, coming from behind, into the back of her head, as she whirled along at sixty miles an hour—and she realized that her teeth were clamped tight, her jaw rigid, as she gripped the steering wheel—

It was intolerable. So as she entered the thickening of habitations which was Larchmont she slowed down to thirty, and two minutes later, arriving at the array of lights from a cluster of filling stations, she slowed still more, rolled on by a short piece, and stopped. When a glance in the mirror showed her that the follower had likewise stopped, the same distance behind as previously, she pushed the gear to reverse and started to back. Back she went, smoothly, alongside the curb, her head turned, her left hand controlling the wheel, until her rear bumper gently kissed the front bumper of TZ9205; then she stopped, pulled the gear to neutral, pulled the hand brake, and switched off the ignition.

A door of TZ9205 was flung open, and she sat motionless, with her head turned again, and stared as Amory Buysse and Woodrow Wilson clambered out and approached her.

"Well!" she said, and breathed deep. "What the dickens do you mean by following me like this?"

The Indian was stretching his wrinkled neck to peer at her from behind his companion's shoulder. Buysse, at the running board, towered above her and had to look down. He said calmly, "We thought we ought to have a talk with you. Right away."

"Did you have to sneak along behind me?"

"I wouldn't say we were sneaking exactly. We just wanted to have a talk with you tonight, and we didn't like to stop you—out on the road like this—"

"What do you want to talk about?"

"Well—" Buysse lifted a foot to the running board and crossed his forearms along the rim of the door. "For one thing, we'd like to ask a few questions about Mr. Guy Carew. Also it might help for you to explain exactly what the hell you were up to there at Barth's place tonight."

"What about Mr. Carew?"

"He's in jail. Arrested for murder."

"I know he is."

"Sure you do. You ought to, you put him there. Who did you calculate you was helping out by telling the cops about his jacket and the yarn and so on?"

"Why, I . . ." Jean was gaping. "I didn't—"

"Somebody did, and you was there. That's one question. The next one might be, is it Wilson here or is it me you're trying to frame for cracking you on the head? You see, ma'am, I'm slow but I'm not crazy. I realize that if they get Guy for the murder, they've got to get someone else for the attack on you Thursday, because he couldn't have done that. After we signed those papers at the dinner table there was some talk about where everyone was. Guy was out of that. We might as well get this settled first, who is it you're trying to frame for it? Wilson or me?"

Jean found speech. "You're crazy. You say you're not, but you certainly are. You've got everything wrong-side up."

"Such as?"

"Everything. I didn't tell the police about the jacket and the yarn."

"Somebody did."

"Certainly. Guy did himself. I was there. They had kept me all night, trying to make me tell, and I wouldn't, and Guy came and told them himself so they would let me go. Also he told them it wasn't true that Portia Tritt had been in his room all the time, and that made his alibi no good, and that was why they arrested him. They didn't put that in the paper. I only tell you because I have—"

"Back up a minute." Buysse was scowling at her. "You say he shed the Tritt alibi? Guy did?"

"Yes. She had lied about it—"

"But he did too. Guy's not a liar."

"No, but he thought that way he could find out—he was being clever."

"He's not clever either."

"Certainly he isn't, but he thought he was. I only tell you about it because I have to tell someone. I'm glad you followed me and I'm glad I stopped. I have to have help. Guy's lawyer is no good, he even thinks Guy is guilty, and he wants me to run away so they can't make me testify about the yarn. I don't even know anything about you, except what I can see in your face, and up to an hour ago I even thought it might have been you who killed Guy's father and knocked me on the head. Now I know it wasn't."

"That's something. How do you know it wasn't?"

"Because I know who it was. I knew by the way he looked at me tonight when the whippoorwill sounded. That may sound silly to you, but I am as positive as if I had seen him do it."

"Maybe—" Buysse's voice was silky. "Maybe you're going to say it was Wilson here."

"No. It was Leo Kranz."

A grunt came from the Indian. Buysse peered in silence at Jean. She said, "I know it was. I'm absolutely sure. But how am I going to prove it? How is anyone going to prove it?"

Wilson grunted again. Buysse finally took a deep breath. He said, "It might be. Kranz. It might be. But you can't prove it by having a man make a noise like a whippoorwill, not even to me."

Jean blurted, exasperated, "Damn it, I don't want to prove it to you! If you're a real friend of Guy's you shouldn't be asking for proof, you should be helping to find it! That's what I was doing when I went to Barth's tonight, and now I don't know what to do next."

"Well, I told you I'm slow. I'm willing to believe you without proof, but that don't get Guy out of jail. I'm no cleverer than he is, never have been, but you seem to tend that way. If you've got any ideas I can help with—"

"I don't know." Jean frowned at him. "I had one and I've used it up. But it isn't possible for a man to do a thing, actually commit a murder, and leave no way of proving it—is it? There are so many things—of course not the weapon, because it was there in the tomb. And no fingerprints, because he wore gloves. And if no one saw him on his way to the tomb or coming back—but there must be something. For instance, the jacket. He must have worn Guy's jacket. He could have got it from the closet in the hall without being seen, but what did he do with it afterwards? He couldn't have returned it to the closet, or the police would have found it; after the yarn was found in Val Carew's hand they searched everywhere for bayeta, so it couldn't have been in the house. And if Kranz hid it somewhere, where did he hide it and why? And how did he get it into Guy's room the afternoon I was there and Guy gave it to me? He wasn't there that day. You see, Mr. Buysse? There's an idea, even if it's nothing wonderful. Where was the jacket from the morning of the murder until the day Guy gave it to me?"

"I had it."

Jean stared, and Buysse jerked around to stare with her, at the Indian. He, in the light from the filling station glare, looked imperturbable.

Buysse demanded, "You had what? None of your damned tricks, now."

"Me?" Wilson grunted. "No tricks. I had the young one's jacket."

"You had it when?"

"All that time. Like she say."

"Where did you get it?"

"It was by me. When my life came to my head that morning. When my life came back I work to get free, first my hands then my mouth then my feet. Then I look around, I see the young one's jacket on the grass under the hedge. Then I see the door open, I go and look, I see Tsianina's man dead. That look good, now he not marry other woman. I go get jacket and shake head at it, I think Tsianina's son big damn fool, after he kill Tsianina's man he leave jacket where anyone can find. Maybe not damn fool, maybe take off jacket when he tie me, then forget so happy when kill Tsianina's man. Leave jacket by so happy forgetting, not by damn fool. I have many cache where I keep things, no one can find. I put jacket in cache, go to house to see young one. Other woman there. He not act big surprise, damn fool again. He send me go tell you—"

"You damn jackass!" Buysse blurted. "All the time you've been sure Guy did it, and I've been sure you did! Is this the truth?"

The Indian shrugged. "Now this woman say Kranz kill Tsianina's man. Good trick. Young one in jail, get him out. Get him out, put Kranz in, everything okay."

"Where did you cache the jacket?"

Wilson grunted. "Maybe show you."

"You bet you will. Did you take it to Guy's room the day he found it there?"

"Me? Sure."

"Why did you do that?"

"Think maybe young one worried where jacket. Me not thief, me not keep anyway. Good day come, take it from cache, take to his room."

"Is this the truth, Wilson?"

"Plenty truth, my friend Buysse. Plenty."

Buysse eyed him a moment in silence, then turned to Jean. "I think it's the truth. I've known him thirty years."

"You see!" Jean put a hand on his arm. "What did I tell you? There's bound to be proof, if only somebody will find it!"

"Well, I wouldn't exactly call that proof that Kranz murdered Val Carew—"

"No, but it helps to prove that Guy didn't! Would he have put his own jacket under the hedge and left it there? And if he had, wouldn't he have asked Wilson later what he had done with it? Wouldn't anyone realize that if he had done the murder and left the jacket under the hedge, then when he found it that day in his room—" Jean stopped with a frown. After a little she went on, "No, that wouldn't fit. It's too complicated for me, at least the way my head is now. I'm about half dead. But what are we going to do about this jacket business and Wilson? Who are we going to tell?"

Buysse slowly shook his head. "Got me. Up to twenty minutes ago I was giving odds that it was Wilson that killed Val, and for a plugged nickel I'd have broke his back for it, but I wouldn't have liked to see the cops get him, and no more would I now. And while this whippoorwill story of yours is good and fancy—"

"It is not fancy! It's absolute fact. And someone has to be told about Wilson and the jacket, but who? Do you know Orlik, Guy's lawyer?"

"I've met him. Got grease in his brains. He made them turn Wilson loose at White Plains."

"I don't care if he did, I don't like him. He wanted me to run away, and anyhow, he thinks Guy is guilty, so he's no good." Jean's frown deepened. "I know another lawyer, but he wouldn't like—I mean, I know him personally." She stopped in perplexity. "It's utterly ridiculous, we've found this out, and what can we do with it? Unless we tell Inspector Cramer." She nodded. "I believe that's it."

Buysse objected, "He'd only lock Wilson up again."

"No, he wouldn't. Not *only* that. I may be naïve, and I've never hated anyone as I hated him last night, but I believe that what he wants is the truth and he'll work to get it. That's the thing to do, I'm sure it is. We'll go to him together in the morning, and take Wilson."

But Buysse balked, and proved to be stubborn. He had various objections, and Jean tried to overcome them. They argued back and forth, with Buysse still unconvinced, and he was finally coerced to reluctant agreement by Jean's ultimatum that she would herself see Cramer in any event, and if she did that Buysse and Wilson would certainly be sent for. She asked Wilson if he would accompany them, and he responded with a grunt which was interpreted by Buysse as an affirmative. It was settled that the two men would call at her apartment at ten o'clock in the morning, Sunday, and they would proceed en masse; Jean gave Buysse her address.

Buysse took his foot from the running board, but turned back to her to observe, "Look here, ma'am, something I think I ought to mention. You've really got it cinched in your mind that Kranz murdered Val Carew. That right?"

"Yes. I know he did."

"That's going pretty strong. There wasn't any whippoorwills in that tomb." Buysse shrugged. "Anyhow, you got a little excited up at Barth's tonight and told him to his face that you knew it was him that cracked you on the head. If it was him that killed Val, he'll figure that you feel the same way sure about that, and being a murderer he'll imagine maybe that you know more than you do, and he might get himself worked up. What kind of a place do you live in?"

"Why—a flat. A walk-up. I told you the address."

"Any men around?"

"In my flat? Certainly not."

"Are you all alone there?"

"At night, yes."

"Well, I don't think you ought to be tonight. You told Kranz right down his throat that you know he's a murderer and you expect to prove it. For instance, I don't think you ought to leave your car in a garage and then go home alone. Wilson and I would be glad to trail along—"

"Nonsense. I'm not afraid. Nothing will happen."

"Really, ma'am, I don't want to—"

"No, thanks very much, it isn't necessary."

She won that argument too, and three minutes later had said good night and was headed south along the Post Road.

She nearly fell asleep in the bathtub. It was well after midnight. The chicken salad which Oletha had left for her in the refrigerator, and the blueberry pie in the oven, had been attacked with ferocity, and had been followed by two cups of tea. The temptation was almost irresistible to fall onto the bed with her clothes on and let blessed sleep take her, but the thought of warm water caressing her skin was seductive too, and she dragged herself to the faucet and turned it on. She would lie there for ten minutes and consider the project of the morning; often while in the bathtub she had got excellent ideas for designs; it seemed to loosen her brain. But it didn't work; instead, she found herself trying to see Guy in jail, the kind of room he was in, what he was sleeping on, if he wasn't sleeping what he was thinking about; then she was dreaming about an enormous door which kept opening and shutting and every time it opened a whippoorwill flew out; and then she was dreaming that she had fallen into a lake of warm milk and someone was pulling her down by the feet and trying to make her swallow the milk. . . .

She jerked up, spasmodically splashing, and spit out a mouthful of the bath water. "Good lord," she muttered aloud, "I might have drowned myself." She opened the valve to let the water out, and stood up and turned on the shower and got it cool. That revived her a little, but as she dried herself and got into pajamas and mules the drowsiness began to return and she realized that she had never been so played out in her life; after all, she reflected vaguely, walking across to the living-room wall switch, there had been that blow on the head. . . .

The doorbell rang. She stopped on a forward foot, startled. At this time of night? Eileen, Oletha? The police? Orlik had warned her that they would be after her again soon, something about a bond. She wouldn't open. Then they might ring all night. Then she would disconnect the bell. There was a short struggle, and curiosity and courage won. She shuffled to the kitchen and pushed the button several times rapidly, and then hastened to the hall to make sure that the door was locked. She stood and listened, and in a moment heard footsteps on the stairs. They approached, without. They halted, and the buzzer sounded.

She called a little louder than necessary, "Who is it?"

"Telegram for Jean Farris."

It sounded like somebody with a sore throat.

She hesitated. "But—why didn't you phone it?"

"Marked for delivery."

Her heart jumped. It hadn't occurred to her, but it was quite possible that people were permitted to send telegrams from jail, especially those who had enough money to bribe somebody—*because I love you*—

She turned the knob of the lock and pulled the door open. A man came in with it, right against her, and she retreated a step, gaping. It was Leo Kranz.

The door was wide-open, and he stood there, in its orbit; then, seeing her immobility, he stepped sidewise, reached for the knob, and swung the door shut. She recovered quickly enough to grab for it, but missed its edge and it banged. She retreated again, two backward steps, stood straight, and told him, "I can scream. If you move I will scream. There are people above—"

"I know there are." He was motionless, staring at her. His voice wasn't steady. It didn't tremble; rather, it vibrated like a tight wire. "There's nothing to scream about, Miss Farris. I only want to talk with you. Just a frank and friendly talk." He moved a few inches forward, she moved as far away, and his lips twisted with a smile. "I didn't give you my name because I knew you wouldn't let me in. Up there tonight I saw you looking at me—and then what you said— you were mistaken. You are making a mistake."

"Open that door and get out. I'll give you five seconds. I'll scream in five seconds."

"You won't talk? Then that means—" His hand stirred; Jean moved; the hand was still again. The wire of his voice tightened: "I tell you you're making a mistake. If I meant any harm to you I could have struck you when you opened the door. I only want to talk—to ask you—"

Probably if he had attacked her that instant, that split second, there would have been no scream, for Jean was momentarily dumb, stunned by a fantastic mixture of physical fear that gripped her stomach and an explosive impulse in her breast to burst into laughter. It had struck her, when his hand moved, that he was wearing gloves. On a warm August night, dressed informally. Dressed for murder. The polite gloves told her politely, "Just in case I do harm you, in case I do have to kill you—" It was funny, pathetic, dangerous—deadly dangerous, like his voice—It was doubtful if he really knew what he was doing—he was desperate—he was a murderer—She would have to scream—she must scream now—even if she screamed he might do it anyway with that stick in his hand—it would be better to leap for him, scratch at him—

The doorbell rang. Kranz's voice stopped, chopped off the tail of a word. She moved—she could back into the kitchen, but she didn't want to leave the hall, that was nearest to the world—she stopped. There was a fainter sound —that was the bell ringing in the flat above—and other faint sounds—someone was ringing all the bells in the house— should she scream now? Instead, she held her breath, and heard the outside door, two flights down, open and close. Then heavy footsteps running upstairs.

Kranz muttered something and made a movement; she paid no attention to it, but stepped forward and seized the knob of the lock and got the door open. The footsteps came nearer, on the second flight, then a man popped up at the stair head and strode along the hall. Below, a door opened and a gruff and angry voice called:

"Who the hell is that? Who rang my bell?"

Jean moved out to the rail and called down, "All right, Mr. Lawson, it's a friend of mine! Excuse it, please!"

She turned, and saw that Kranz had stepped out too and stood there facing Amory Buysse. Neither man said anything. Kranz turned to her:

"You're quite popular tonight. And all the commotion— really—" He took a step.

"Wait a minute." Buysse was in front of him. "How about it, Miss Farris? Do you want him for anything?"

Kranz said, "I came to see Miss Farris. I wanted to have a talk with her."

"All right, go ahead and talk."

"No." It was Jean. "There's nothing to say. We'll wait here until we hear the door close behind you downstairs."

Kranz stared at her, then turned without a word and went. Buysse followed him, five steps behind, down both flights, and saw him leave and heard the door click, and then went back up. Jean, standing in her door, said, "Come in." Then, inside, she closed the door, took him to the living room, and sat herself on the edge of a chair.

Buysse said apologetically, "I followed you again, but not so close. I figured that if Kranz killed Val he must be half crazy and he might do anything. I guess now he really did. I was hanging around across the street—"

"God bless you. Where's Wilson?"

"Over at my place asleep. What did Kranz say?"

"Nothing." Jean, sitting on the edge of the chair, shivered convulsively. "He just said he wanted to have a talk with me."

"Why did you let him in? I mean up here."

"He disguised his voice and said it was a telegram. I thought maybe it was from Guy. Then he stood . . . he said I was making a mistake." Another shiver ran over her. All at once she giggled. She bit her lip, gazing at Buysse, and giggled again. "He had on gloves! Did you notice? Gloves!" She burst into laughter. "Isn't that a scream? Isn't that *funny?*" Her head went back, then forward; the laughter was a rushing crescendo. "Gloves!" She rocked back and forth, the laughter rocking with her.

Buysse scowled down at her. "God blame it," he muttered, "she'll wake the whole damn block." He strode to the kitchen,

138

came back with a glass of cold water, and dashed it into her face. She gave a gasp and slumped in the chair and the laughter stopped.

Twenty minutes later she was in her bed sound asleep, and Buysse was on the couch in the living room with his shoes off, wiggling his toes in the dark.

XVII

At half past nine Sunday morning Amory Buysse, with his face washed, his hair combed, and his shoes on, sat at the little table in Jean Farris's living room enjoying his second cup of coffee, having consumed two dishes of sliced peaches and cream, and four fried eggs with toast. He was enjoying the coffee, but was nevertheless glowering at the tablecloth, for he was far from easy in his mind. He had told this stylish young woman that he and Wilson would go with her to Police Headquarters, and they would; but he didn't like it. If he had ever seen a cop that looked like a cop, it was Inspector Cramer; and in his opinion the cop who had put Guy Carew in jail was a hell of a man to go to, to help get him out. He was wishing to God he had been born clever.

The door to the bedroom opened and Jean appeared. She had been up since eight; had prepared the breakfast—since Oletha didn't come on Sunday—and eaten her share of it; had phoned three times to Inspector Cramer's office; and had been at average pains to produce the sartorial effect which she now displayed. Her summer dress, cream-colored with tan stripes, was topped by a hip-length jacket of the same material, her straw falcon hat, the tan of the stripes, was at an angle that stopped before it touched the tilt of freakishness, and her brown suede pumps clicked with modish Dorlan heels.

She approached the table demanding, "What do you suppose happened to Wilson? We mustn't be late. Didn't he say he was ready to leave?"

Buysse set down his empty cup and nodded. "He'll be here. We'll make it all right. Probably he's walking to save taxi fare—he sure hates to turn loose of money—there he is now."

The bell had rung, and Jean hurried to the kitchen to push the button. Buysse got up and went to the hall to open the door. Jean started on a trot to carry the dishes out, but on her second trip stopped with the coffeepot and sugar bowl in her hand at sound of a voice she didn't know. After leaving them in the kitchen she went to the hall. Wilson, the Indian, grunted at her and she grunted back; and in the doorway stood a stranger who was telling Buysse:

"Yes, sir, I know, but I had to see you. I tried to get you on the telephone last evening and couldn't, so this morning I came in from Lucky Hills and went to your rooms and Mr. Wilson was there just ready to leave, and he said he was going to join you, so I took the liberty—"

"Well, right now I'm going somewhere." Buysse turned to Jean: "This is Richards, Val Carew's valet. Guy has kept him on at Lucky Hills—what is it, Richards? Can you make it short?"

The man hesitated, glancing at Wilson and Jean. He was tall, narrow all the way up, with colorless eyes and not enough flesh to round out his cheeks, which in another hour at the most would be needing a shave. He stammered, "I'm afraid I can't make it very short, sir. It's quite—personal. I wouldn't like—with other people—"

Jean said brusquely, "He can wait here till we get back."

"All right, Richards? Will it keep?"

"How long will you be, sir?"

"Oh, maybe a couple of hours. Maybe more. Cut out the sirs. I don't like 'em."

"Yes, sir." Again he hesitated. "The fact is, I've worked myself up to do this. It's really quite shameful. Absolutely shameful. I should hate to have to sit here—if there is any way of avoiding it—"

"Who's it shameful to?"

"To me, sir."

"What's it about? Has it any connection with the murder of Val Carew?"

"I hope not, sir—I sincerely hope not. But there is that to be considered, and that's why I came—"

Jean put in, "I said we'd be there promptly at ten, and it's a quarter of. Listen, Mr. Buysse, I'll go along with Wilson, and you come as soon as you can."

Buysse frowned. "I don't like the idea of Wilson—"

"It's all right." Jean moved. "I can take care of him as well as that lawyer could. You come as soon as you can. Be sure the door's locked when you leave." She touched Wilson's elbow. "Come on."

The Indian grunted, and followed her.

Inspector Cramer sat at his desk with a mangled cigar between his teeth and watched the door close behind the departing Sergeant Burke. To his left, across the desk from him, Woodrow Wilson sat, in blue overalls and blue shirt with red tie, the slits of his eyes only two more wrinkles among the ravines of his leathery old face; to his right Jean Farris, though not so picturesque, was just as certainly a picture.

Cramer said, "You'll have to make it snappy. I'm seeing you only as a favor. The Carew case is back in the hands of District Attorney Anderson of Westchester County, where it belongs. But just as a favor to you, Miss Farris—what's on your mind?"

Jean took a breath, looked him straight in the eye, and said, "One thing is that I know who killed Valentine Carew."

"That's pretty good for a start." Cramer wasn't impressed. "Who was it?"

"Leo Kranz. Also he hit me on the head Thursday evening and took my clothes. Also he intended to kill me last night, and he probably would if Mr. Buysse hadn't come."

Cramer studied her a second, then leaned back. "Listen, Miss Farris. I've got an appointment at 10:30. You have no idea of the number of goofy stories that have been told in this room, and the amount of rambling I've had to listen to. I didn't have you down for goofy, and I wouldn't have thought you were a rambler. If you really have got something you should take it to District Attorney Anderson, that's where it belongs, but I'll take it if it's short and to the point. First, Kranz murdered Carew. Go ahead."

Jean shook her head. "No, first he hit me. I mean I'll tell you that first. There at Barth's Thursday, I was lying on my back on the grass with my eyes closed, right at the edge of a thicket. Suddenly there was a loud shrill sound, it seemed right at my ear, and I jerked up, sitting. It was a whippoorwill. Just as I realized what it was, the blow came. When I came to my skirt and jacket were gone. You know about that."

"Yeah, I know."

"Well, yesterday afternoon I was trying to think of some way I could do something, and it occurred to me that I hadn't mentioned the whippoorwill to anyone. No one knew about it. I decided to try an experiment. I phoned Mrs. Barth and made arrangements, and I got hold of a man who could imitate a whippoorwill and took him into Barth's place without anyone knowing he was there. Last evening at dusk I went to the same spot by the thicket with Mr. and Mrs. Barth, Mr. Buysse, Mr. Wilson, and Leo Kranz. I took them there on a pretext—it doesn't matter. They were all close to me, looking

141

at me as I talked, when the sound of a whippoorwill came from right behind me, from the thicket. They were all startled and looked around. The call of a whippoorwill is very loud and startling when it's that close. But I wish you could have seen Leo Kranz. After a fraction of a second he turned and looked directly at me, and the expression in his eyes was plain as words, 'What's this, a trick?' That's exactly what his eyes said, and no one else looked at me at all, they were looking for the whippoorwill."

Jean leaned forward, and her voice trembled with earnestness: "I know it, Inspector, I absolutely know it, it was Leo Kranz who hit me!"

Cramer grunted. "Done with that?"

"Why—yes."

"Then Kranz murdered Carew. Try that one."

She shook her head again. "That comes last. And I said —they were looking for the whippoorwill—and one of them found it. Buysse. He dragged the man out of the thicket, and I had to admit I had brought him, and I was excited and I told them that I had learned who had attacked me at that spot. Kranz already knew that anyway, from the way I looked at him when he looked at me, or at least he suspected it. Then I took the man away and put him on a train at Rye and went home. After I had eaten something and taken a bath it was past midnight. I was just going to turn off the light when the doorbell rang. I punched the button for downstairs, and when I asked through my hall door who it was he said a telegram. I opened the door and it was Leo Kranz. He pushed in and closed the door. He had gloves on. He said he wanted to have a talk with me, that I had made a mistake, but the way he looked and the tone of his voice—if you could have seen him and heard him—"

Cramer was frowning. "What do you mean, he had gloves on?"

"I mean he had gloves on! An August night, and he was dressed in an ordinary sack suit, the same one he had worn at Barth's. I know it sounds silly sitting here telling it, but he had gloves on because he didn't want to leave fingerprints at my flat. And he had his heavy walking stick."

"What happened?"

"Buysse came. He had followed me—I had had a talk with him and Wilson and told them about Kranz—and he had followed me and was watching across the street. He rang the bell, all the bells, just as I was going to scream, and he came up and I opened the door—and Kranz said he had only wanted to talk with me and went away."

142

Cramer said drily, "Buysse was on the job, wasn't he? By the way, I thought you said he was coming here with you."

"He'll be here later."

"Okay, go ahead."

"You . . ." Jean gazed at him. "You're so cold!"

"Yeah, I know. I used to get overheated. This case is something special for you, Miss Farris. For me it's just part of the twelve hours. It has to be, or I wouldn't last. Go ahead. I'll comment when you finish."

"I guess that's all." Jean forced her voice to be calm and businesslike. "I mean, all the facts. I didn't tell you I could prove it was Leo Kranz, I only said I know it was. It's obvious that if he attacked me Thursday evening, he murdered Val Carew. He had learned on Tuesday that a piece of the yarn had been found in Val Carew's hand, and he heard me say there at Barth's that the yarn in my suit had come from the jacket, and he wanted to destroy it so it couldn't be traced—"

"It wasn't his jacket, it was Guy's."

"But he had worn it! He must have! He could have got it from the hall closet as easily as Guy, couldn't he? He did it deliberately, so he could leave it under the hedge and throw suspicion on Guy. Then when he learned—"

"Wait a minute. Leave what under what hedge?"

"The jacket. I'll come to that later. When he learned that Guy was out of it on account of the alibi Portia Tritt gave him, he was frightened. He was already uneasy because the jacket hadn't been found, as he had expected it to be, and with Guy safe from suspicion he was frightened, and when he learned that a piece of the yarn was found in Val Carew's hand he was in a panic. So at Barth's that day, when he heard that the bayeta yarn was in my suit, he was in still more of a panic, and he saw me going across the grounds and followed me, and knocked me unconscious and took the suit. Another thing, Guy couldn't have done that. At the time I was attacked he was talking to a group of people on the terrace."

"Wilson or Buysse could have done it for him."

"Me? Damn fool."

They were both startled; they had forgotten the Indian's silent presence. Jean ignored his contribution: "They could have, but they didn't, because I know it was Kranz." She spread her open hands. "Inspector, listen to me. I know I can't prove Kranz killed Carew. I can't prove anything. But haven't I told you—isn't this enough to make you doubt Guy's guilt? To make you think about it, to work at it?"

Cramer shook his head. "It's not my case any more, Miss Farris."

"You made it your case to put Guy in jail! Can't you make it your case to get him out?"

"The lawyers get 'em out, I don't. My job is to get 'em in."

"The right ones or the wrong ones? Don't you care which?"

"Sure, I care." Cramer slowly scratched his head. Finally he heaved a sigh. "I promised to comment. Well, you haven't said a thing with any nourishment in it. Yesterday I gave it as my opinion to the commissioner and the district attorney that there was enough evidence to convince a jury of Guy Carew's guilt, and if I was asked for it again now I would repeat it. I like you, Miss Farris. Usually I get sore at people who hold out on me, it's part of my make-up, but I didn't get sore at you Friday night. I liked you then, and I like you now, and that's why I'm not a damn bit comfortable this minute, whether I show it or not. I think Guy Carew killed his father, and I think it can be proved that he did. You don't agree with me, and that's natural, but it makes me want plenty of corroboration for any statement you make."

Jean met his gaze with her lips pressed tight together. He tossed his mangled cigar into the cuspidor and went on, "And what is it you tell me? That you saw a look on Kranz's face when a man made a noise like a whippoorwill! Maybe you did and maybe you didn't; you're in a good condition for imagining things. Then you tell me Kranz came to your apartment and got in by saying he was a telegram, and he had gloves on because he intended to kill you, and Buysse appeared and saved your life. But all Kranz said was that you were making a mistake and he wanted to have a talk with you. That right? Did he attack you? Did he put a hand on you? Do you claim that he even threatened you?"

"No. Not in words. But if you had seen him—"

"But I didn't. And you know as well as I do that you're in no state of mind to see straight or hear straight. If I was inclined to bear down, I might make it stronger than that. I've seen desperate people before, and some of them just as likable people as you are. You've admitted that you hadn't mentioned about the whippoorwill to anyone. Maybe because there wasn't one? You sat around yesterday afternoon trying to think of something to do, and maybe you thought of the whippoorwill gag, and frankly, I think you might have done better. It's too fancy—"

Jean flared. "But I—I wouldn't *lie* about it!"

"No? You wouldn't? Do you mean to tell me you wouldn't think up a lie if you thought it would save Guy Carew from the electric chair?"

"But I didn't have to—"

"But would you?"

Jean met his eye. "Yes, I would. Of course. But not a lie that would implicate anyone else. Never. And I am implicating Leo Kranz."

"You sure are trying to. And I don't know, maybe I'm too old and got too thick a crust, maybe you can make a dent in Anderson up at White Plains. Go on up and try. He'll see you; in fact, he intends to see you, and I'm surprised he hasn't done so already. But if you want some unofficial advice, what you had better do is try it on Carew's lawyer. Sam Orlik knows how to make use of anything, even a whippoorwill." Cramer glanced at his watch. "And now—I'm sorry, but I've got an appointment—"

"But I'm not through." Jean sounded determined, and looked it. "There's something else—and you can't say it's my state of mind or accuse me of lying about it, either. Because it's a fact. I know where the jacket was from the morning of the murder until the day Guy found it in his room and gave it to me."

"Yeah? Where?"

Jean turned to the Indian. "You tell him, Wilson. Tell him about the jacket."

The Indian stirred a little, then was immobile again. The dry rattle sounded: "Me. I have jacket."

The inspector's eyes shot to a new target. "Where is it?"

Jean said impatiently, "He means he had it."

Wilson asserted imperturbably, "I say I have it. My words no good?" He grunted scornfully. "I have jacket many days. When my life come back that morning I work free I look around I see jacket on grass under hedge. I see tomb door open and go and find Tsianina's man dead. I not like jacket there, too much around, I hide him. Then I go tell Tsianina's son what I find in tomb. After many days, fifteen days, it come like lightning in my head, why, sure, I know about that jacket. That jacket belong Tsianina's son. Of course. Damn fool. I get jacket from cache, put it in his room on chair. Of course. Happy to remember."

"I see." Cramer, pulling thoughtfully at his lip with a finger and thumb, said that and stopped. He sat and stared at the wrinkled old face, his own forehead wrinkled as though in violent distaste. Finally, still staring, his hand reached out for the button on his desk, found it and pushed.

In a moment the door opened to admit Sergeant Burke.

Cramer said crisply, "I'll be busy here a little longer. Tell McConnell to take those two men, separately of course, and get going. He'd better start with Pinkie Frick. I'll join him as soon as I can."

"Yes, sir. There's a man out there that wants in. His name is Amory Buysse. He just came."

"Keep him until— No. Send him in."

"There's another man with him, I don't know who he is."

"He can wait. Send Buysse in."

"Yes, sir."

The sergeant went. No one spoke. It was a minute before the door opened again and Buysse appeared. He crossed, glanced at Jean and then at Wilson, and looked without marked friendliness at Cramer.

"Good morning, Inspector."

"Good morning. Pull a chair up."

Jean blurted, "Inspector Cramer says I'm lying about the whippoorwill and that Kranz came to my apartment last night just to have a talk."

Buysse sat down and put up his brows at her. "Well, you wanted to come here. I knew that was about what you'd get."

Cramer declared, "Miss Farris is exaggerating. Anyhow, we've passed that." He turned to the Indian: "Now you. You know what I can do to you if you tell me lies."

Wilson shrugged. "No lies. Plenty truth."

"Okay. You say that when you came to that morning you were bound hand and foot. You worked yourself free, and looked around, and saw the jacket under the hedge. After you had gone to the tomb and saw what was there, you hid the jacket before you went to the house to see Guy Carew. That right?"

The Indian grunted.

"Then, fifteen days later, you got the jacket from where you had hid it and took it to Guy Carew's room and left it there in his absence. Right?"

Another grunt.

"How do you happen to remember it was exactly fifteen days?"

Buysse said shortly, "That's your ignorance. Indians always count days for everything."

"Good. Good thing you're here, Buysse, much obliged." Back to Wilson: "How did it happen that you didn't tell the police about the jacket?"

"No one speak of jacket. No one ask."

"I'm aware of that. That was their ignorance. Why didn't you speak of it?"

"Not here." With his middle finger Wilson tapped his temple, then flipped the finger to the wind. "Clear out."

"Why did you hide it?"

"Not hide to keep. Me no thief."

Cramer's voice went up a little. "Why did you hide it?"

"Habit of Cherokee Indian. Everything put away."

"That's fine. And you say you didn't know whose it was, and fifteen days later it popped into your head like lightning that it belonged to Guy Carew, so you got it and took it—"

Jean broke in, "That's silly! It's perfectly obvious why he said that, and why he hid it! Because he knew it was Guy's jacket, and he thought Guy had killed his father, and he wanted to shield him! He told Mr. Buysse and me that last night—that's when we learned about it. There's no sense in bullying him about anything as obvious as that." She got up and went over and put her hand on the Indian's shoulder, and bent down to face him. "Listen, Wilson. Don't be afraid of anything. Don't be afraid of the truth. The truth is going to come out, and we want you to help with it. Don't be afraid of it. I think it was wonderful of you to try to shield Tsianina's son; it was beautiful. Do you know the word beautiful?"

"Sure. Sun, water, fast cloud—"

"That's it. It was beautiful. And I promise you that no harm will come if you tell the whole truth—if you will accept my promise. I don't know much about a Cherokee Indian's opinion of a woman, I've only read about it in a book. Will you trust a woman?"

He shrugged. "Trust one day maybe. Find out."

"Well, make it today. You can trust me, I swear you can. I swear it! Do you know what it means when I swear?"

"Sure. Goddam hell and Jesus—"

Cramer snorted. "Okay, Miss Farris. Fine. Did you rehearse it?"

She straightened and wheeled. "Rehearse what?"

"Oh, the little act. Sentiment and humor all together— very pretty. My God, do you think I'm a ninny? This isn't any better than the whippoorwill—in fact, it's even worse. I get the idea, of course. If Wilson found the jacket under the hedge it couldn't have been Guy who left it there, because he wouldn't have been fool enough to leave his own jacket on the scene. I'll admit there's a little subtlety to it, but—"

Astonishment stopped him, for Buysse suddenly roared, "Shut up!" Then Buysse turned to Jean: "I said he was a cop, didn't I? He's a cop and he acts like a cop."

Jean, disregarding him, was standing against the edge of the desk, as close as she could get to Cramer, facing him, her eyes flashing. "Yes," she told him scornfully, "you are a ninny! You are a complete fool! You had the nerve to say you like me. God help the people you don't like! You have accused me twice of lying, of deliberately making up things. You accuse me of inventing this story for Wilson. Good Lord, if Buysse and Wilson and I wanted to invent something, couldn't we do better than this? If we were willing to endanger a man who might be innocent? I can invent one right now. When Kranz left the tomb after murdering Carew, Wilson wasn't still unconscious; he only pretended to be. He opened his eyes enough to see Kranz going by and leaving through the gap in the hedge, after he had put the jacket there on the grass. He has kept still about it up to now because he was afraid to talk. Also Buysse, out of his bedroom window, saw Kranz going toward the tomb and coming back again, and he has kept silent because he didn't want to testify against an old friend. How do you like that?" She hit the desk with her fist, and her eyes blazed. "I could do much better if I had ten minutes to think it over! And you are stupid enough to accuse me of making that up for Wilson! And of inventing the whippoorwill in an effort to put it off on Leo Kranz! You *are* a ninny!"

Silence, except for Jean's breathing.

The Indian muttered, barely audible, "Maybe good woman."

Buysse said, "Sit down, Miss Farris. Sit down and cool off."

Cramer stirred in his chair. At length he conceded, "Okay. As Buysse says, I'm a cop. I'll string along with the Indian, maybe good woman."

Jean was still glaring at him. "Do you believe me? Do you believe everything I've told you?"

"Now don't shove. My capacity for believing people ain't what it used to be. Let's say you've made a point, I'll agree to that. Sit down, and we'll—what do you want, Wilson?"

The Indian had reached forward to tug at Jean's sleeve. She turned to face him. He looked up at her:

"You say tell truth. All truth?"

"Yes, Wilson, all of it. Everything."

He peered up at her, and she let her eyes meet him straight. At length he nodded as if satisfied, looked at the inspector and spoke:

"Okay. Damn fool maybe. In tomb I see Tsianina's man

148

on floor dead. I lift one eye more open, dead. I think he forget Tsianina, daughter of chief, he look at other woman, now dead. I happy to think, very happy. Then I think young one do good maybe. Then I think fact about Cherokee life. Old far life, gone. I happy to think. I get knife, real Cherokee knife, I scalp Tsianina's man, first time I scalp, come off hard. I put scalp in belt of old Cherokee chief on wall. I go out, wash hands in dew, hide jacket, go to see young one." He grunted. "Plenty truth."

Buysse was looking at him disapprovingly, with compressed lips. Jean had backed off a step. Cramer gazed and said, "Well, by God."

Wilson observed, an afterthought, "Knife plenty dull."

Buysse muttered at him, "You damn old cuss." He turned to Jean: "You win as far as I'm concerned. Kranz did it. I couldn't swallow it before, because I simply couldn't believe that he had taken that scalp. I know, he might have done it to throw suspicion on Guy or Wilson, but even so I couldn't believe it. But by persuading Wilson to tell the truth you've fixed him. He committed a crime. They call it mutilating a corpse."

Jean shivered. Cramer growled, "I'm not interested in mutilating a corpse." He glared at Wilson. "Damn you, anyway, and your plenty truth!" He glared some more, in silence. Suddenly he arose, pulled a jackknife from his pocket, opened the large blade, walked around the desk, and extended the knife in his hand.

"Here. You say you scalped Carew? Show me how you held the knife."

Wilson grunted. "How you think? Teeth maybe? Damn fool." He took the knife and gripped its handle. "I hold him that way."

"Yeah?" Cramer's eyes narrowed. "And you scalped him, and put the scalp in the belt of that outfit on the wall, and threw the knife down—"

"Me?" The dry rattle was contemptuous. "Head full of rabbit soup? You think? Take doeskin moccasin, wipe fingerprints from knife. Put back moccasin, knife on floor."

"How did you happen to think of fingerprints?"

"Movies." Wilson shrugged. "See movies two days every week. Movies full of fingerprints. You know?"

Cramer looked disgusted. He took back his knife and snapped the blade shut, and returned to his chair. Jean, sitting again, jabbed at him, "I suppose I invented that too."

Buysse observed, "That seems to settle the scalping. You

thought an Indian scalped him. All right, an Indian did. But an Indian didn't kill him."

"So you say," Cramer snapped. "You say Kranz did it. Huh? For what? He had been a close friend of Val Carew's for fifteen years. So he murdered him for the lousy quarter of a million legacy he would get? No. Kranz is worth a million or more himself, and his affairs are in good shape."

"It wasn't that," Jean blurted. "It was Portia Tritt."

"What about her?"

"Carew was going to marry her."

"Baloney. Kranz killed his old friend because he didn't want to lose a good publicity agent?"

"Of course not. He killed him because—" Jean stopped short.

"Well? Because what?"

Jean shook her head. "I—I shouldn't. Everything else I've told you, I know, but I don't know this. It's only gossip."

"Then I'll take it for gossip. If you mean he was in love with her, her lover maybe, naturally we've thought of that but we haven't got anywhere with it. Is that what you mean?"

She shook her head again, more firmly. "I won't talk about it. I shouldn't have said what I did, because I don't really know it."

"Suit yourself." Cramer glanced at his watch. "I'm late. I'll give you folks some good advice. You've cooked up a nice mess of hash, and the best thing you can do is go and dump it on Sam Orlik. He's Guy Carew's lawyer and he has a right to it. I was chiefly responsible for this charge against Guy Carew, and I still think he's guilty, but I have no more desire—"

"You *can't* think he's guilty!"

"Pardon me, Miss Farris, but I sure can, and I do." Cramer leaned towards her and extended an upturned palm. "Now look here. Use some common sense. You seem to have an idea that you came here this morning with evidence. Evidence of what? I mean evidence for a court and a jury, or even for a prosecutor. Nothing whatever. For the sake of argument, let's say you've got me believing that Kranz killed Carew. You haven't, but let's say you have. Let's say I'd like to go to District Attorney Anderson and tell him that I think I made a mistake and that Guy Carew is innocent and Kranz is guilty. Anderson asks me why. I tell him. First, the whippoorwill stunt, for which we have only your word, and it can't be corroborated. Second, that Kranz went to your apartment wearing gloves and said he wanted to have a talk with you. Third, that Wilson found the jacket under the hedge and hid it. Fourth, that it was Wilson who scalped Carew."

Cramer spread out both hands. "Wouldn't I make a hot impression with that? Anderson would have me committed for lunacy! And here, let me put it another way. Let's say that Kranz is actually guilty, he really did kill Carew, and I'm convinced of it and want to prove it. I'm telling you straight, I wouldn't know where to start. There's not a shred of evidence against him. I'm not saying he couldn't have done it, I'm only saying there's nothing whatever to show that he did, whereas there are four damaging and conclusive proofs that Guy Carew did. I mean conclusive enough for a jury—"

"Back up a minute." It was Buysse, wearing a scowl. "You say there's no evidence against Kranz or anyone but Guy. If I present you with a little scrap, will you follow it up? You personally?"

"I've already said, Mr. Buysse, it's not my case—"

"I know, I heard you, and I heard Miss Farris's reply, and I think it was a good one. I'm not offering anything to brag about, but it's a fact I don't think you know, and I think you ought to hear it. The reason I'd rather have you hear it than Orlik is because you've got official investigating power, and he hasn't. Will you follow it up yourself?"

"I'll tell you that when I hear it."

Buysse tightened his lips. Then he opened them again: "All right. I wish to God there was some place to take it besides here. I brought a man down here with me. His name's Richards, Val Carew's valet. He's outside. Have him brought in here."

XVIII

Clarence Richards was obviously scared. He sat on a chair which had been placed between Jean and Buysse, and gulped every few seconds, with his colorless eyes fastened on a corner of the inspector's desk and his hands twisted together in his lap. Nor did he seem to be able to speak at the first invitation.

Cramer demanded impatiently, "Come on, Richards. Let's hear it."

He stammered, "I didn't think—the police—"

Buysse was impatient too: "Didn't I tell you the police can't touch you unless there's a complaint, and there won't be any?"

"Yes, sir." He gulped again. Then he looked at a button on the inspector's vest and plunged: "I promised Mr. Buysse to tell you about the impression of the key Miss Tritt wanted me to get."

"Okay." Cramer's eyes narrowed. "Shoot."

"Well—" Another gulp. "It was in June, the last Saturday in June. Miss Tritt was at Lucky Hills for the weekend. She came to me—she said she supposed I would be putting out Mr. Carew's clothes while he was in the bath, and I said yes. She said she supposed I knew that Mr. Carew carried the key to the tomb in a special pocket on his belt and I said yes. She said she supposed his belt would be with me putting the clothes out and not in the bathroom and I said yes. Then she offered me a hundred dollars if I would make an impression of the key on some wax she had, and I said no. I was very much shocked."

He glanced from right to left, but there was no vocal commiseration for his shock, so he assaulted the silence again: "That evening she came back to me. She offered me one thousand dollars. I said I would think it over. I didn't promise, I just said I would think about it. I got to thinking about my radio. I had a radio in my room, an old seven-tube Hostetter, and a new Clarkson had just come out, the very finest on the market, and I had seen one and been permitted to try it during a visit to New York—its price was three hundred and fifteen dollars—"

Cramer grunted. "Did you take the impression of the key?"

"Yes, sir. Yes, sir, I did. Two of them."

"With the wax Miss Tritt gave you?"

"Yes, sir."

"When?"

"Sunday morning, sir."

"Did you give her the impressions?"

"Yes, sir."

"Did she pay you the thousand dollars?"

"Yes, sir. Not all at that moment. She gave me two hundred, and the balance the following Wednesday."

"What did she want to get into the tomb for?"

"I don't know, sir. She said she would do no harm, that she only wanted to prepare a surprise for Mr. Carew, but it would be of such a nature that he would never know she had been there, and there was no chance of his discovering about my—my co-operation. I would never have done it if I had thought there could be harm in it."

"Sure you wouldn't. Then what?"

"Nothing, sir. That was all."

"Do you know how often she used her duplicate key or when she used it?"

"No, sir, I know nothing about it." For the first time Richards' eyes met those of the inspector. "But I repeat, sir, I believed her assurance that no harm would be done. She was very direct about it, very convincing. Do you know the lady, sir?"

"I've met her."

"Yes, sir. As I say, that was the last weekend in June. So it was just nine days later that Mr. Carew was murdered in the tomb. I was very much shocked. I thought about it, I sat in my room thinking about it. It didn't seem possible that Miss Tritt had done it, and anyway, the murderer hadn't used a key to get into the tomb, because Mr. Carew was already in there. But I had had strong regard for Mr. Carew, he had been very good to me, and I felt very miserable about it. I decided I must tell someone. I thought perhaps I should tell the police, but I didn't want to, and what I finally did, I went to Mr. Kranz and told him everything and asked his advice."

"Why Mr. Kranz?"

"Well, he was Mr. Carew's oldest friend. He had been there often, for years, and I thought—"

"Did he give you any advice?"

"Yes, sir. He remarked about the murderer not using a key, and said it would be very embarrassing for me to tell the police, which of course agreed with my view. He said he would consider it, and if it seemed necessary to inform the police he would do so himself and save me the embarrassment. He was very kind."

"He sure was. Then what?"

"Nothing, sir. Nothing at all. I don't know whether he told the police or not. I was never approached."

"I approached you myself Friday morning. Day before yesterday."

"Yes, sir, of course. I mean—"

"I know what you mean. If nothing else happened, why did you come here today?"

"But something did happen, sir. I came here because Mr. Buysse insisted on it. Yesterday afternoon, as soon as I learned that Mr. Guy Carew had been charged with murdering his father and put in jail, I was very miserable again. I began thinking again. It looked very uncertain whether I had gone to the right place for advice when I went to Mr. Kranz. I knew that at one time he had been extremely intimate with Miss Tritt, for once at Lucky Hills I had seen them clasped in each other's arms, kissing and so on—"

"When was that?"

"Last summer, sir. Nearly a year ago."

"Did you see that more than once?"

"No, sir. In a way, you might say, if you will pardon the freedom, once was quite enough."

"Okay. And Guy Carew's arrest got you thinking again?"

"Yes, sir. I didn't know Mr. Guy very well, I had seen little of him, but when I heard he had been arrested I was very much shocked. I felt sure that Mr. Carew would not have wished his son to be suspected of killing him. I still could not believe that Miss Tritt had lent herself to murder, but after all the key she got was for that tomb, where the murder was. So I felt I should have more advice, and since Mr. Guy was in jail the only one left was Mr. Buysse. I tried to telephone him last evening from Lucky Hills, but there was no answer, so this morning I came to town to see him. He was very kind, but he insisted I should come here."

Richards hesitated, then went on, "There is one thing, sir, I should like your opinion on." He reached in his pocket and pulled out a bulky envelope. "I have six hundred and three dollars and fifty cents left of that money, after buying the radio and a few odds and ends. I brought it with me. What would be the ethical thing for me to do with it?"

"Stick it—" Cramer stopped himself. "Here, give it to me. You'll get a receipt for it. It may be wanted as evidence. Did I hear you say that Mr. Buysse told you that the police can't touch you?"

Buysse broke in, "You did. I wanted to get him down here. His offense was against Val Carew, and he's dead. I undertook to guarantee that Guy will make no complaint."

Cramer grunted. He sat a moment regarding Richards, and then asked him, "You never saw the key Miss Tritt had made from the impressions you gave her?"

"No, sir."

"You have no idea whether she had it made or used it?"

"No, sir."

"Are you ready to swear that you took the impressions at her request, and gave them to her, and she paid you for them?"

"If I have to, yes, sir."

"I mean, what you've told me is the truth? Every word of it the truth?"

"Yes, sir."

"And you've held nothing back?"

"No, sir."

"If I bring Miss Tritt here, will you repeat your story, just as you have told it, in her presence?"

Richards squirmed. But almost at once he nodded firmly. "Yes, sir. I should hate to, but it's my own fault. On account of that radio. Yes, sir."

The inspector turned abruptly to Buysse. "You win," he snapped. "Maybe this has nothing to do with the murder, in fact I would offer odds that it hasn't, but I'm going to follow it up for my personal satisfaction. No woman is going to make a monkey out of me if I have anything to say about it. I may need Richards later on, so I'll keep him for the present—"

"I'll keep him for you, Inspector."

"Much obliged, but I'll attend to it." Cramer reached to press the button on his desk.

Buysse shook his head. "No, I'll keep him. You see, I gave him a promise and I'd like to keep that too. We'll be around, no matter when you want him. All of us. We have nothing else to do, and we'd like to keep sort of in touch with the situation. If you don't mind."

Cramer grunted. The door opened, and Sergeant Burke entered. Cramer addressed him:

"I want Portia Tritt and Leo Kranz here as quick as you can find them. If they balk, take them as material witnesses and no apologies. When they come, keep 'em separated, and let me know. I'll be in McConnell's room." He got up.

Burke glanced around. "Any of these—"

"No. They're just slumming." The inspector stalked out.

XIX

Commissioner Humbert sat and looked glum.

District Attorney Skinner stood with his back to a window, his hands thrust into his trouser pockets, and told Inspector Cramer in an energetic and belligerent tone:

"You admit yourself that it probably has nothing to do with the murder. Damn it, all I'm asking for is a little discretion, a little regard for realities. Portia Tritt is no particular friend of mine, but she knows a lot of people and they're making my life miserable. I repeat, Cramer, you can't treat people of standing and influence like you treat a bunch of gangsters. You simply can't get away with it. Another thing. I'm called in from the golf links to the telephone to hear the pleasant news that you've hauled in Portia Tritt again as if she were a bag of potatoes, and I break my neck getting down here, and what do I find? After digging up evidence against Guy Carew and persuading Anderson to paste a murder charge on him, which alone is a ton of dynamite—"

Humbert put a hand up. "Now wait a minute, Skinner. Be fair. Cramer didn't persuade us to arrest Carew. He placed the evidence before us, and the decision was made by all four, including Anderson."

They were in the commissioner's spacious and comfortable office, at three o'clock Sunday afternoon, with the shades drawn to exclude the hot August sun. Humbert, who had breakfasted at noon at the Churchill, had a highball at his elbow on his desk; Skinner had finished one; Cramer, who had lunched on salmon sandwiches and milk in McConnell's room, joining in the attack on Pinkie Frick between bites, had refused his and continued to chew on a cigar.

The district attorney shifted to an aggravating tone of pained remonstrance: "I am willing to concede, Inspector, that Miss Tritt was difficult in her interview with you yesterday, but it's our business to deal with difficulties in a diplomatic manner. Certainly we should never permit our personal feelings to become engaged, no matter how trying the circumstances, and I strongly suspect that you are bearing Miss Tritt a grudge merely because she was—er, guilty of a misrepresentation. I assure you I am not trying to suggest—"

"Nuts."

"I beg your pardon?"

"I just said nuts." Cramer took his cigar from his mouth. "I'm not a microphone, I'm only a police inspector. You don't have to make a speech, just say what you mean, that people who are in a position to make trouble have to be handled differently from those who aren't. I know that, and I try to string along, whether I like it or not. I have to. Sure, I admitted this probably has nothing to do with the murder, but it was in the investigation of a murder that Miss Tritt concealed something that we had a right to be curious about, not counting her phoney alibi for Guy Carew. Also I admit my personal feelings are a little bit engaged; I'm a man and I've got 'em. But the chief point is this: How would you like to have the Carew case go to trial, and the state's case in and the tabloids hitting new circulation highs, and then explode and blow the roof right off the courthouse? I know it's Anderson's case, not ours, but we wrapped it up and delivered it to him, and everybody knows it. That's what's on my mind ahead of any personal feelings. Yesterday I would have given 100 to 1 that Guy Carew was guilty and could be convicted. Right now I'd give 93 to 1, or maybe 92. I don't like the loss of that 7 or 8 points, and my intention is to look into it."

Cramer stuck his cigar in his mouth and took it out again. "The commissioner here is my superior officer. If he orders me to apologize to Miss Tritt and send her home, I'll—I'll send her home. Otherwise I'll ask her some questions, and I'll get answers."

"I haven't suggested that you send her home! It's perfectly proper to question her, of course! I only say—"

Humbert broke in, "Why don't both of you cut it out? Good God, it's after three o'clock! Where is she, Cramer?"

"Third floor."

"Is Kranz there too?"

"Yes."

"Well, have them brought down here. Both of them."

"I strongly advise—I want her first."

"Do you really think it's as important as that?"

"No, sir. But it may be."

Humbert picked up his highball, and sighed. "All right. Send for her."

Cramer went to the telephone on its bracket and asked for Extension 19.

Portia Tritt wore a dull-green street dress, of very simple cut, with hat and pumps of black patent leather and a black lightweight summer wrap, faced with the dull green of the dress. She came in a few paces and stopped. Cramer and Humbert arose. Skinner crossed to her and they shook hands. Commissioner Humbert was introduced, and a chair was placed for her. She was quite gracious and amiable, considering the serious inconvenience she had been compelled to submit to. Cramer sat again, with his lips screwed up. Skinner took a chair to her left and told her:

"Dick Elliott phoned me and I came right down. We're sorry you had to wait so long, but the inspector was busy with some malefactors and we didn't dare interrupt him."

She smiled. "I imagine the inspector deals with so many malefactors that he hardly knows how to act with commonplace people like me." She turned to Cramer, with the smile intact. "Isn't that so?"

Cramer unscrewed his lips. "Maybe it is, ma'am. I'd never thought of it." He turned to the commissioner. "Do I proceed, sir?"

Humbert nodded. "Go ahead."

She repeated the smile. "More questions, Inspector?"

"Yeah, a few." He shifted in his chair to face her better. "I'm going to begin, Miss Tritt, with a couple of remarks. The district attorney here has just accused me of having personal feelings about you, meaning that I'm sore. All right, I am, I admit it, and I'd like to explain why. You gave us a phoney alibi for Guy Carew. Okay. I've busted hundreds of phoney alibis, it's part of the day's work. Yesterday afternoon you made it tough going for me every step of the way, and I wasn't sore about that; I hadn't supposed you were a jellyfish. But I gave you a good deal. You could have been held and charged without any trouble at all, but I let you go. This minute you could be and you should be out on bail, bonded for an appearance, but I let you go. In spite of that, what do you do? Two things. First, you get a bunch of your friends to phone the mayor and the commissioner and the district attorney and maybe the superintendent of sewers in an effort to tie knots in my tail. My tail don't bend that easy. Second, even worse, when you left my office yesterday, going with no strings attached on account of my generosity, you were still holding out on me. So I'm sore, I admit it, but I didn't get you down here to satisfy a personal grudge. I sent for you to tell you that you're through holding out. This time I want all the facts you've got."

Portia Tritt smiled at him, let the other two have a taste of it, and then gave it back to the inspector. "Really," she said, "I'm over thirty years old. You'd find some of my facts pretty dull."

"We'll skip those. We'll skip all that aren't connected with the Carew murder. Here's the first one I want: What did you do with the duplicate key you had made for the door of the tomb Carew was found murdered in?"

The smile disappeared. It didn't return; but her composure did, short of two seconds. Her voice was almost good enough: "What makes you think I had one?"

"Not any personal feeling," Cramer asserted drily. "Maybe you think I was trying to take you by surprise, but I wasn't, because I don't have to. I'm not really asking you for facts, because I already have them; what I want from you is an explanation of them. On Sunday, June 27, nine

158

days before Carew was killed, Richards, his valet, gave you two wax impressions of the key to the tomb. You had furnished the wax. You paid him two hundred dollars, and a few days later you paid him the balance to make up the thousand you had promised. Right?"

The smile was gone for good. One of her hands was clenching the edge of the black and green wrap. She swallowed before she said, "No."

He shook his head. "No good, Miss Tritt. Richards is upstairs. Shall I have him brought down here?"

"No."

"But I'll have to if you don't admit it, which is the only sensible thing for you to do. Did you—no, wait a minute. I'll empty the whole bag for you. I'll admit that I have no proof that you actually had a key made. So I'll ask you that. Did you have a key made from the wax impressions you bought from Richards?"

"No."

"Okay." He turned abruptly to the commissioner. "I wish to detain Miss Tritt in custody—remembering that she was responsible for the fake alibi for Guy Carew—until tomorrow noon. At eight in the morning I'll send out squads with photographs of that key to all locksmiths she would be likely to go to. By ten o'clock we ought to know who made one for her."

Humbert frowned. Skinner demanded, "Why keep her in custody? She won't murder the locksmith. I thought you had proof—"

Cramer, disregarding him, addressed his superior: "May I keep her?"

Humbert pursed his lips. Then he leaned forward: "Look here, Miss Tritt. Don't be stubborn when it can't help you. If you did have a key made we're bound to know it by noon tomorrow, and you won't have helped yourself any by the delay. Inspector Cramer was perfectly correct when he said he was generous to let you go yesterday. I'm afraid you can't count on much more generosity. If you did have a key made I would certainly advise you to say so. Did you?"

She looked at him, but not at Skinner. After a moment she jerked her shoulders back, breathed, and turned to the inspector. "Yes," she said.

"You got a key to the tomb?"

"Yes."

"When did you use it?"

"I never used it."

"What did you get it for?"

"I got it—" She swallowed. "What I got it for has nothing to do with the murder you are investigating. It was—it was silly. Just something to surprise and please Mr. Carew. It was purely personal between him and me."

"What was it?"

She shook her head. "I assure you—I give you my word—it had nothing to do with the murder."

"Will you tell what it was?"

"No."

Cramer leaned back with a sigh. "You make it tough, Miss Tritt, and you really shouldn't. We might all be out of here, and you on your way home, in five minutes, if you'd say what it was and get it over. Since it had nothing to do with the murder. You see, you're in this thing. You're in it for good. You'll be on the stand at Guy Carew's trial, there's no way out of it. If you tell us now when and why you used that key, and it had no connection with the murder, it won't come up at the trial at all, and will never be made public. If you don't tell us, you'll be questioned about it on the stand. If you tell on the stand, you may or may not be believed because there'll be no chance to check up. If you refuse to tell on the stand, everybody, including the judge and jury, will think the key was connected with the murder, and you may find yourself on the spot."

Portia Tritt's eyes were intent at him. She said calmly, "They can't think the key was connected with the murder. The door was unlocked when the murderer went in."

"Who said so?" Cramer demanded. "That has been the assumption up till now, because no one knew anything about a duplicate key. It wouldn't be hard to suppose that the murderer got there before Carew did, knocked the Indian out and bound and gagged him, let himself into the tomb and locked the door on the inside—"

"No," the district attorney put in. "Carew would have seen—"

Cramer cut him off with a murderous glare. "Damn it, is this a departmental conference or an investigation?" He returned to the charge: "I don't know if you are aware, Miss Tritt, that your attempt to manufacture an alibi for Guy Carew has already put you in a difficult position. That's a mild word for it. People don't often hear gossip about themselves, so you may not have heard the latest public morsel, that you and Guy Carew conspired to kill Val Carew so you two could get married and enjoy the fortune—"

"That's a lie!"

"I expect it is. But you're not in much of a position to get

160

indignant about a lie. And you must admit it's logical. If you add to the other facts a new one, that you got a key to the tomb and refuse to tell what you used it for, I tell you frankly, it may get to be worse than gossip." He leaned to her. "You haven't asked for my advice and maybe you don't want it, but take it from me, you are already carrying a peak load on this murder and another few pounds might break your back."

He straightened, shrugged, and said as one who had made all possible concessions, "Thank God it's your back and not mine."

Portia Tritt wet her lips, and sat motionless, her chin up, regarding him. No one said anything.

Cramer spoke again: "Another thing apparently you don't understand. Mr. Skinner here is district attorney for New York County. This isn't a New York County murder, it's Westchester. If you are held on charges, anything from murder accomplice down, it won't be Mr. Skinner who will prosecute you, it will be Anderson of Westchester, and I don't think he—"

"I resent that!" Skinner interrupted hotly. "I resent the implication—"

"You've got nothing to resent," Cramer retorted. "I'm addressing myself to a misconception Miss Tritt may have in her mind. She don't seem to realize what she's up against. You know what Anderson himself said here in this room yesterday noon. I'm stating a plain fact when I say that if Miss Tritt adds concealment about this key to that fake alibi, it's better than an even chance that she'll be locked up on a charge of complicity in murder. I ask you, is that true?"

Skinner looked sour. Portia Tritt wet her lips again. She turned to the district attorney:

"Is that true?"

Skinner finally nodded. "I'm afraid it is."

"That I—arrested for *murder?*"

"Complicity—legally it's the same thing."

"And if I tell now what I did with the key, I wouldn't have to tell it again"—she shivered—"on the witness stand?"

"Probably not, if it wasn't connected with the murder." Skinner was frowning at her. "If your use of that key had a possible relation to the murder, I would advise you to submit to arrest, get a lawyer, and leave it to him. If it had nothing to do with the murder, tell us about it now. And if you do tell us, it will be best not to overlook any details. I don't know what information Inspector Cramer already pos-

161

sesses, but you can be sure that every word you say will be rigorously investigated."

Her shoulders were drooping and her chin was down. No one had her eyes; her gaze was apparently directed at the toe of her patent leather pump. At length, and slowly, she returned it to meet the unrelenting steady regard of the inspector.

"All right," she said calmly. "I used the key. I got in the tomb with it."

"How many times?"

"Once."

"Only once?"

"Yes."

"When?"

"Tuesday afternoon, the day before Val Carew was killed. A little before four o'clock that afternoon. At that time the old Indian was always in the house taking a nap, and I knew I wouldn't be seen."

"What did you do in there?"

"I—" She stopped and glanced around, at Humbert, at Skinner, and back at Cramer. "I know what you've been thinking, naturally. That my getting that key had some connection with the murder, but it hadn't, none whatever. I haven't wanted to tell it, and I still don't want to, because it will sound ridiculous, and I don't like to sound ridiculous any more than most people. Even less, I suppose. But in fact it wasn't ridiculous, it was sensible and practical. I went to the tomb to put paper in the holes in the wall so the sun couldn't come through."

Humbert's chair creaked. Skinner stared at her with his brows up. Cramer asked, "Did you do it?"

"Yes. I took some Pasilex—"

"What's that?"

"A cleaning tissue made of very soft paper. That's the kind I use. I took some, and stuffed it into three of the holes, because I wasn't sure which one the sun would come through the next morning, though you could tell pretty accurately, standing on the platform. Then I went out again and back to the house. That's all I did. I wasn't in there more than five or six minutes."

Cramer's eyes were narrow. He said, stating a fact, "You couldn't reach the holes from that platform."

"Of course not," she agreed. "Not with my arm. But— I've told you that Val Carew had taken me there the Sunday before, to show me the tomb. The idea of shutting out the sun had occurred to me before, and that was why I had persuaded him to take me inside, so I could look at it in advance. I saw that there were lances on the wall with which I could reach the holes from the platform, and that's what I used, one of the lances. I put a piece of Pasilex on the tip of the lance and pushed it in. I used nine pieces of Pasilex, three in each hole." She smiled, with no humor, at the inspector. "Now, of course, you've caught me in another lie. I said that the fingerprints that were found were put there on the day that Val Carew showed me the tomb. That was true about those on the top of the relic cabinet. But the ones on the lance handle and the glass lid of Tsianina's casket and the lever of the door were put there that Tuesday."

Cramer grunted. "Have you still got the key?"

"No. I put it under a stone in the brook."

"Could you find it?"

"Easily."

"This was on Tuesday afternoon, July 6th?"

"Yes."

"And you left the Pasilex stuffed in the holes? It was still there when you left the tomb?"

"Certainly. That was what I went there for."

"How far in did you stuff it?"

"Not far. Just in the entrances of the holes."

"And did you think that would deceive Carew? Didn't you realize he would know if the sun was shining outdoors, and if it didn't come through to Tsianina's face he would look at the hole, and would be unable to see daylight through it, and would see it was stuffed with something?"

"Of course I did. But I knew a good deal about how he felt about it. It was a genuine superstition with him. The whole point, the only point, was whether the sun did actually enter and shine on Tsianina's face. If you are genuinely superstitious about thirteen at table, it doesn't remove the curse to know that someone deliberately arranged to make it thirteen. Besides that, he did want to marry me. He wanted to—very much. We had discussed this, and he had as good as told me that interference by a—by any agency, would not invalidate the verdict. The only question was whether or not, for those few moments, the sun entered."

"You mean he practically invited you to interfere."

"I didn't say that. But it almost amounted to that. You can verify it if you want to, because one of those discussions was in the presence of a mutual friend, Leo Kranz."

"Yeah? Kranz, huh?"

She nodded. "He'll verify it."

Cramer looked at her in silence, with his lips screwed up.

Finally he heaved a deep sigh, and shook his head. "Well," he declared, "I'd have thought you'd learned better sense. Didn't Mr. Skinner advise you not to overlook any details, meaning you'd better tell the truth?"

"I understood it that way. I have told the truth."

"Oh, no, you haven't." Cramer's voice took on an edge. "You have told an absolute barefaced lie! You have said you stuffed the Pasilex in the holes Tuesday afternoon, and left it there, and didn't go back! Then what became of it? The police got there at eight o'clock Wednesday morning, and they examined every inch of that tomb, and there was no Pasilex in the holes or anywhere else! Pasilex hell!" He leaned to her, and his eyes were menacing. "I can't rough-house you, I know that, so what you'd better do is get a lawyer and dig in. Let him juggle your lies a while. What I'm going to do right now is phone Anderson of White Plains and advise him to give you room and board as an accomplice in first degree murder!"

He was on his feet, and she put out a hand to stop him.

"No! Wait!"

He whirled on one foot and glared. She appealed, "I haven't lied! I've told the truth! The police didn't find it because it wasn't there any more! It had been taken away!"

"Who took it?"

"Leo Kranz."

"When? Did he have a key to the tomb too?"

"No." She was more composed. "He didn't need one. That morning—when Val was killed—when Guy went to the tomb he took Leo along. Surely you know that. Guy left Leo there and went to the house to telephone. Leo was there alone, and he looked around, and saw something was stuffed in the holes. He got a harpoon from the wall and pulled the stuff out and saw what it was and kept it. He—he knew it was mine because it was yellow Pasilex, and he knew I used that, and it isn't very common."

Cramer, still standing, demanded savagely, "What did he do with it?"

"He took it. He kept it."

"Has he still got it?"

"Yes. He did have, two days ago. That was when I learned he had taken it. He told me. I had been wondering what had happened to it—I had been wondering why the police hadn't found it, and learned it was mine—and asked me about it. Leo sent me—I went to see him, and he told me about it."

Cramer sat down, very deliberately. He took a cigar from his pocket, frowned at it as he rolled it between his

164

fingers, and then stuck it in his mouth and clamped his teeth. With slow ferocity he chewed.

Skinner asked irritably, "Time out for a cud?"

Cramer ignored him. After a while he removed the cigar and addressed the commissioner: "I'm on a line, sir. May I follow it?"

Humbert, with sharp eyes on him, merely nodded.

Cramer got up and went to the phone on its bracket and spoke into it. After a little wait he spoke again.

"Burke? Send Leo Kranz to the commissioner's office right away. You might bring him yourself, you need the exercise."

XX

Leo Kranz, with admirable control of his temper, smiled.

Inspector Cramer had made changes in the seating arrangement. He had requested Portia Tritt to move to another chair at the district attorney's left, keeping the one she had vacated for Kranz. This put Kranz next to him, and also had the advantage that Portia Tritt would be on Kranz's left and somewhat to his rear as he sat facing the inspector. Sergeant Burke, requested to remain, had a position against the wall.

Kranz said with his smile, "I've been kept incommunicado up there for four hours, and I was prepared to make a row. But when I see that you gentlemen are missing your Sunday too, I realized it must be important, and—" He shrugged. "Of course it's this dreadful business—I've never been as horrified in my life as I was when I heard that Guy Carew had been arrested."

They nodded. Cramer asked, "What's your opinion of it, Mr. Kranz? Do you think he's guilty?"

"No, I don't," Kranz said firmly. "I simply can't believe it. Of course if you have proof, real proof—and I suppose you have or he wouldn't have been arrested. . . ."

"Yeah. I just wondered how you felt about it." Cramer got rid of the cigar. "There's one or two little questions I want to ask you. For instance, on various occasions you have been asked if you knew anything that might have a bearing on the murder, and you have always said no. Why didn't you tell us that Miss Tritt had a duplicate key to the tomb?"

Kranz's eyes flickered. His head started to turn for a glance at Portia Tritt, but seeing that he would have to go

165

more than ninety degrees to make it, he gave it up. "Why," he said with composure, "that seems apparent, doesn't it? There wasn't the slightest reason to suppose it had anything to do with the murder."

"Then you admit you knew about it?"

"Certainly." He smiled. "Since obviously you know all about it."

"All or part. When did you first learn of it?"

"The day after the murder. On Thursday. Richards, the valet, told me what he had done and asked my advice."

"And you told him to keep it quiet and didn't see fit to mention it yourself?"

Kranz upturned a palm. "I've explained, haven't I, Inspector? There was no earthly reason to suppose it was relevant to your investigation. I confess I was reluctant to involve Miss Tritt in unnecessary unpleasantness."

"Did you know what Miss Tritt had used the key for?"

"No."

"Do you know now what she used it for?"

"No."

Cramer grunted sarcastically. "You lie like a gentleman. We know all about it."

Kranz's eyes narrowed a little, and for a moment he was silent. "In that case—" he began, and stopped; and this time his head went around far enough to bring Portia Tritt into his line of vision. She was sitting properly and still, her little pumps decorously side by side, ankles touching, on the Velatan rug which was the commissioner's personal property, her shoulders up, her hands clasped in her lap; but any familiar acquaintance would have wondered why her lips were so tight. No sudden gleam or shadow in her eyes acknowledged Kranz's glance.

Kranz returned to the inspector and finished his sentence. "In that case, anything I might tell you would be secondhand."

Cramer shrugged. "I'm not trying any tricks. I don't have to. One thing about us cops, Mr. Kranz, we have an idea that anything done around the scene of a murder, especially shortly before or shortly after, may be both relevant and material and we have a right to be told about it. It's an idea that has often been tested, and we find it pays to hang onto it. We don't want to involve Miss Tritt in unnecessary unpleasantness any more than you do, or anybody else, but we don't like to leave loose ends hanging to make a tangle later on. For instance, what if Guy Carew's lawyer finds out about this key business? We want to know at least as much about it as he does, and we wouldn't mind if we knew more. And frankly, since you were an old friend of Carew's, we figure he'll probably know about it, and we want to know too. Miss Tritt has kindly given us a lot of information, and with no disrespect to her, we want to check it. That's natural, isn't it?"

Kranz smiled a little. "I suppose it is. But I maintain I had no reason to suppose it relevant—"

"Okay." Cramer waved it away. "Now, Miss Tritt tells us that she used the key to get into the tomb Tuesday afternoon, the day before the murder. She had with her some pieces of a cleaning tissue called Pasilex, and she took a lance and stuffed them into three of the holes in the wall so the sun couldn't get through to shine on Tsianina's face. As she says, it may sound ridiculous, but it was really sensible and practical. After the murder, she naturally began to wonder why the police hadn't found the Pasilex, and she kept on wondering. She couldn't imagine what had happened to it. Two days ago she found out, when you told her that you had it. You had removed it from the holes in the wall yourself, with one of the harpoons in the tomb. Is that correct?"

Kranz nodded. "Yes."

"Then—I don't want to overlook anything—why didn't we find your fingerprints on the harpoon handle?"

Kranz smiled. "Because I wiped them off. It was the scene of a murder, and I didn't care to explain what I had been doing with the harpoon. As I said, I didn't want to involve Miss Tritt—"

"Yeah, I remember that. How did you know the stuff was hers?"

"Why—" Kranz hesitated. He lifted his shoulders and dropped them. "That's a luxury article, quite expensive, and not many women use it. I happened to know that Miss Tritt did. Also it was yellow, which is the shade she uses. Also she was present, there at Lucky Hills."

"So you felt sure it was hers as soon as you saw it?"

"Yes."

"How did you happen to see it up there in the holes?"

"I was looking around. Guy had left me there alone while he went to the house to telephone. After the first shock of seeing Val there dead, I investigated a little. I examined the floor, and looked around, and went up the steps to the platform where Tsianina's casket was. Standing on the platform, I looked at the holes, and I noticed that by stretching my neck I could see daylight, the bright sky, through two of the holes that I could line my eye up with, but not through

167

the three nearer ones. The light was dim, but it looked as if there was an obstruction in the entrance of the holes. I went down and got a harpoon from the wall and went back up and poked carefully, and pulled the stuff out. From all three holes. I wiped off the harpoon handle and replaced it, and picked up the pieces where they had fallen to the floor. I took them to the door, to the light, and saw what they were. Naturally I was astonished. I was considering what to do, when I saw Buysse coming, and I stuffed them into my pocket."

Cramer looked stern. "Mr. Kranz, you were deliberately removing evidence from the scene of a murder."

"I know I was. I don't pretend it hasn't bothered me, because it has, but it seemed to me a justifiable thing to do, because it was inconceivable that it was in any way related to the murder. Certainly Miss Tritt had not killed Carew."

"Nevertheless, you were violating a law, and making for yourself a decision which was the function of the police. You say you stuffed the Pasilex into your pocket?"

"Yes."

"Which pocket?"

Kranz put a hand on his right thigh. "This one. My side trouser pocket."

"You're sure of that?"

"Certainly." Kranz raised his brows. "Those moments made an indelible impression, Inspector."

"Yeah, I suppose they did. You told Miss Tritt two days ago that you still had the Pasilex. Have you got it now?"

Kranz smiled. "Not with me."

"Where is it?"

"At my home."

"Whereabouts at home? You see, Mr. Kranz, I want that Pasilex. Whether it's evidence of anything about the murder or not, I don't want anyone else to have it, and the safest way to avoid that is to get it myself. Will you give it to me?"

Kranz was frowning. "I don't like to."

"Why not?"

"Well—there is still the question of involving Miss Tritt—"

"She can't be more involved than she already is. My possession of the Pasilex won't hurt her any. Of course we can get it with a warrant, but why force us to take that trouble? Where do you keep it at home?"

"I—" Kranz stopped. Then he shrugged. "In my bedroom. I have a small safe there."

"Much obliged. Now to go back a minute. You say that

there in the tomb you put the Pasilex in your side trouser pocket. Right?"

"Yes."

"That was when you saw Buysse coming?"

"Yes."

"A little later Guy returned. And soon after, a few minutes past eight, the police came. Correct?"

"Yes."

"From the time Buysse came until the police arrived, did you go outside the tomb at all?"

"Outside the tomb?"

Cramer nodded. "I mean leave the tomb. Go outdoors."

"No."

"Or while the police were there?"

Kranz frowned. He lifted his head a little, slowly. "Why, I went eventually, of course—"

"Yeah, I know. Around nine o'clock you and Guy went to the house with Captain Goss. I mean, did you leave the tomb between the time the first cops arrived and the time you left with Guy Carew and Captain Goss? I know you didn't, I've read the reports and I know 'em by heart."

"Then why the devil do you ask me?"

"Because I like to check things. Did you?"

"No."

"And when you left the tomb with Guy Carew and Captain Goss, and went with them to the house, the Pasilex was in your side trouser pocket?"

There was no answer. Something was happening to Leo Kranz. The blood was leaving his face, his lips were parting, and the tips of his fingers were digging into his legs.

Cramer went on inexorably, "And it had been there all the time, undisturbed."

Kranz was white, his mouth open, speechless. Portia Tritt got up and took three steps to stare at him. The others stared from their seats. Sergeant Burke moved brusquely from the wall.

Cramer asked in a tense voice, "Got it at last, have you? It took you long enough! But you finally got it, huh?"

Skinner demanded irascibly, "What the hell did he get?"

"Plenty," said Cramer grimly. "As that Indian says, plenty truth. He couldn't have found that Pasilex when Guy left him in the tomb, and put it in his pocket and kept it there, because when the cops came he was searched, and searched good. There was only one other time when he could possibly have got it, and that's when he did get it—when he went to the tomb before, earlier that morning, and murdered Val Carew!"

Portia Tritt sank back into her chair.

XXI

It was close to six o'clock when Inspector Cramer left the elevator at the third floor and tramped down the hall to the entrance to the homicide bureau. From the side of his mouth a cigar was tilted well on its way to the perpendicular. He entered the office and was making a beeline across the anteroom when out of the side of his eye he caught a glimpse of something that stopped him. He wheeled, looked a moment, and ejaculated:

"For God's sake! Have you folks signed a lease?"

The Indian, who had been stretched out on three chairs, slowly raised himself, blinking. Clarence Richards, confined to one chair, didn't move. Amory Buysse lifted his eyes from a magazine. Jean Farris moved her head a little; she was seated next to Buysse, her shoulders sagging, her eyes lifeless.

Cramer demanded, "Have you been sitting here all afternoon?"

Buysse shook his head. "We went out for a bite to eat." He put the magazine down. "We saw Miss Tritt going through here around three o'clock, and Kranz over an hour ago. You didn't send for Richards."

"I didn't need him." Cramer had crossed to them. "I got along without him."

"You got along?"

"Yes. It's sewed up. Thanks to you folks. Especially you, Miss Farris. I guess you're part bulldog. Anyway, you were right. It was Leo Kranz. It's him that's sewed up."

Buysse stood, kicking his chair back. Wilson yawned. Richards raised his colorless eyes, looking very shocked. Jean gasped, "What?"

Cramer nodded. "It was Kranz who killed Val Carew. As near as I can see, Guy is out of it and so is everybody else. Anderson's on his way down here now to get Kranz."

Buysse said, "You sure changed your mind in a hurry."

"Yeah, I know." The inspector looked down at Jean. He opened his mouth and closed it; then opened it again and got it out: "Any time you'd like to have a medal, Miss Farris, let me know and I'll arrange it. You're okay. I've got a daughter in High School and I'm going to tell her about you. I think kids ought to have ideals."

Jean rose to her feet, but her knees buckled and she sat down again. The color had left her face, but was coming back. "I guess," she said, "I've been sitting down too long." She tried a little laugh, but it was squeaky. "Do you mean it's all over? You can prove it wasn't Guy? It's all over?"

"That's what it looks like, yes, ma'am."

"Well." Jean sat gazing up at him. Suddenly she jumped to her feet. "Well!" she cried. She wheeled to the Indian: "Did you hear that, Wilson? Am I a good woman?"

Wilson grunted. "Damn good maybe," he conceded.

She pivoted to Cramer. "You did it! You believed me all the time! You did it!" She faced him, her hands up to his shoulders.

Cramer blushed. "Well," he admitted, "a notion did finally come to me—"

"Of course you did it! I knew you would! And I'd like to—you say you have a daughter? Send her to me, right away, tomorrow, and I'll take her to Krone and she'll have the swellest fall outfit in New York! I'll design it right on her! If you want to come along I'll design something on you too!" She giggled.

Buysse took two strides and reached to pluck her sleeve. "Now here," he commanded firmly, "don't you get started laughing—"

Wilson yawned.

XXII

Monday afternoon, two hours after lunch, Jean was perched on the high stool at the big table, frowning with disgust at an enormous sheet of squared paper which didn't have a mark on it. Two chronological facts were in a bitter struggle for the front of her consciousness: (1) that it had been six days since she had done a lick of work; and (2) that it had been twenty-two minutes since he had telephoned to ask if he might come. She was tapping against a pin rack with a large red crayon. The door behind her opened. She hastily started to pretend she had been using the crayon on the squared paper, then with a derisive grunt threw it down, and turned the stool on its swivel.

Guy Carew said, "Hello, here I am."

Jean slid from the stool and met him, extending a hand. "Well!" She tried not to wince at the squeeze he gave her hand, and said "Well!" again.

Not being able to think of anything more to say, she returned to the stool and sat on it and looked at him. He sat down on a chair and looked at her.

She said, "You don't look—you look quite fresh."

He nodded. "I had a bath and a change. You look—you look all right."

"Thanks. Did you say you were phoning from your lawyer's office? I thought that was near here somewhere."

"It's over at Forty-third and Madison. The crosstown traffic was terrible. I left the taxi and walked."

"Sure." She nodded in sympathy. "The traffic."

"Yes, it's terrible." He crossed his legs and uncrossed them again. "Orlik—that's the lawyer—he was telling me some things he had just learned from Inspector Cramer. One thing I thought would interest you—about the jacket. You remember I left it in a closet in the hall when I came in from the tennis court? Portia Tritt has admitted that later that evening, when she went outdoors, she wore that jacket, and when she came in she left it in the upstairs hall in the north wing. That explains how Kranz happened to be wearing it. He just saw it there and put it on. I suppose he got the idea later of leaving it out there by the hedge because he knew it was mine."

"I suppose so. I suppose you feel pretty sorry for Portia Tritt, don't you? I do."

"Yes. I feel sorry for everybody, including Kranz. I feel particularly—it's my fault that you were dragged into this—"

"Forget it," Jean said brusquely. "Was it pretty bad up in that jail? Dirty?"

"No, it was quite clean. There was a strong smell of disinfectant, but that was better than dirt."

"Did you—could you sleep?"

"Towards morning I slept some. They let me smoke cigarettes until ten o'clock. Then I lay on the cot and thought about you. I said some poetry to myself about you. I'm not very familiar with the kind of poetry you would know, but I'm an authority on Indian poetry. Some of it I've had a real feeling for, and some of it I haven't, but I have a new feeling about it now. For instance, this song from the Haida, translated by Constance Lindsay Skinner:

> "'Beautiful is she, this woman,
>   As the mountain flower;
>   But cold, cold, is she,
>   Like the snowbank
>   Behind which it blooms.'"

"You didn't——" Jean stopped to swallow. "You didn't say that to yourself about me!"

"Yes. Many times."

"But that's absurd! I'm not at all cold!"

Guy shrugged. "I don't think it means cold in a general sense. I'm sure it meant a specific coldness to the Indian who sang it centuries ago; it meant that he loved the beautiful woman but she didn't love him. That's what it meant to me last night. Then there was a Shoshone love song, translated by Mary Austin:

> "'Neither spirit nor bird;
>   That was my flute you heard
>   Last night by the river.
>   When you came with your wicker jar
>   Where the river drags the willows,
>   That was my flute you heard,
>   Calling, Come to the willows!
>
> "'Neither the wind nor a bird
>   Rustled the lupin blooms,
>   That was my blood you heard
>   Answer your garment's hem
>   Whispering through the grasses;
>   That was my blood you heard
>   By the wild rose under the willows.
>
> "'That was no beast that stirred,
>   That was my heart you heard
>   Pacing to and fro
>   In the ambush of my desire,
>   To the music my flute let fall.
>   That was my heart you heard
>   Leaping under the willows.'"

Jean said a little faintly, "Well . . . that Indian knew how to make love. It was a Shoshone who sang that? What would a Cherokee sing?"

Guy, looking into her eyes, and seeing but not believing, stammered, "I sang—I said—a Cherokee song too, but I couldn't say it to you now because it boasts—it is the song of a lover who had won—" He stood up, pulled up by her eyes.

She said, "Sing it now—come here, Guy—sing it now—Guy!"

He sang the boastful Cherokee song a little later.

Brand New Inexpensive Editions... The Most Thrilling

SPY STORIES
Come From Pyramid!

ASSIGNMENT K by Hartley Howard   X-1737/60¢
A tense spy thriller of a double agent and a triple cross—now a major motion picture.

THE 9TH DIRECTIVE by Adam Hall   T-1734/75¢
Smash successor to THE QUILLER MEMORANDUM. Secret agent Quiller duels with a deadly Mongolian assassin in Bangkok. "Best counter-espionage novel of today"—**Publishers Weekly**

THE INVISIBLE EYE by Paul Tabori   X-1728/60¢
A monstrous criminal scheme against humanity is foiled by the dedicated group of HUNTERS. Second in a popular series.

THE COUNTERFEIT TRAITOR by Alexander Klein   T-1722/75¢
The most dangerous spy of World War II... an incredible true story of espionage at its most daring.

COMMANDO X by Poke Runyon   X-1693/60¢
The private army whose dedication to the overthrow of Castro could explode into world war!

THE VENGEANCE MAN by Manning Coles   X-1631/60¢
Tommy Hambledon's most bizarre case in which the action begins in Montmartre and reaches a stunning climax on the coast of Spain.

THE QUILLER MEMORANDUM by Adam Hall   T-1570/75¢
The most widely read and admired espionage novel since THE SPY WHO CAME IN FROM THE COLD and FUNERAL IN BERLIN. "Best spy novel of the year"—The New York Times.

TONGUE OF TREASON by Robert Crane   R-1633/50¢
Special agent Ben Corbin faces diabolical killers and swinging spy girls in this spy thriller.

NOTE: Pyramid pays postage on orders for 4 books or more. On orders for less than 4 books, add 10¢ per copy for postage and handling.

------WHEREVER PAPERBACKS ARE SOLD OR USE THIS COUPON------
PYRAMID BOOKS Dept. 202, 444 Madison Avenue, New York, New York 10022
Please send me the SPY STORIES circled below. I enclose $_____.

X-1737   T-1734   X-1728   T-1722   X-1693   X-1631   T-1570   R-1633

Name _____
Address _____
City _____ State _____ Zip _____

NEWEST MYSTERIES
to keep you guessing!

ROCKET TO THE MORGUE by Anthony Boucher   X-1681/60¢
A baffling yarn about murder among science fiction writers in Southern California, by The New York Times mystery reviewer.

THE NAME IS JORDAN by Harold Q. Masur   R-1714/50¢
Ace lawyer-detective Scott Jordan unravels a series of murderous and legal dilemmas in this sparkling anthology.

A MASK FOR THE TOFF by John Creasey   R-1540/50¢
The Toff, gentleman-adventurer, plays a double game of disguise, danger and death in an underworld war.

THE NAME IS MALONE by Craig Rice   R-1729/50¢
John J. Malone solves some of Chicago's most baffling murders in this collection of his most interesting cases.

THE CASE OF THE SOLID KEY by Anthony Boucher   X-1733/60¢
The glamour of Hollywood and the dazzle of high-powered detection make this one of Anthony Boucher's best and most deceptive bafflers.

THE NAME IS CHAMBERS by Henry Kane   X-1738/60¢
Private-eye Pete Chambers is called in to solve killings which have left the cops high and dry.

**THE CASE OF THE CRUMPLED KNAVE by Anthony Boucher
R-1585/50¢**
Two ingenious and quite different sets of clues make this mystery "cleverly constructed, neatly solved"—*The New York Times*.

**THE CASE OF THE SEVEN SNEEZES by Anthony Boucher
R-1542/50¢**
Death from the past means murder tomorrow! "Super-tense and startling" —*Saturday Review*.

NOTE: Pyramid pays postage on orders for 4 books or more. On orders for less than 4 books, add 10¢ per copy for postage and handling.

—WHEREVER PAPERBACKS ARE SOLD OR USE THIS COUPON—

PYRAMID BOOKS
Dept. 205, 444 Madison Avenue, New York, N.Y. 10022

Please send me the MYSTERIES I have circled below. I enclose $_____.

X-1681   R-1714   R-1540   R-1729   X-1733   X-1738   R-1585   R-1542

Name_____

Address_____

City_____ State_____ Zip_____